Jan. 17, 2019,
Canada Game Pool.
10:38 am
@ hot tub.

Sutra of the Medicine Buddha
with
an Introduction, Comments and Prayers
by Venerable Master Hsing Yun

藥師經及其修持法門

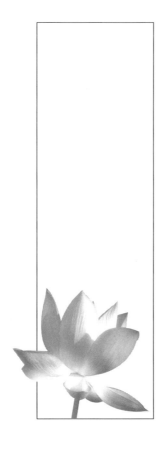

©2002 Buddha's Light Publishing

By Venerable Master Hsing Yun
Translated by Fo Guang Shan
International Translation Center
Edited by Brenda Bolinger
Book and cover designed by Mei-Chi Shih

Published by Buddha's Light Publishing
3456 S. Glenmark Drive,
Hacienda Heights, CA 91745, U.S.A.
Tel: (626) 923-5143 / (626) 961-9697
Fax: (626) 923-5145 / (626) 369-1944
e-mail: itc@blia.org

ISBN: 0-9715612-9-x

Library of Congress Control Number: 2001099616

Contents

Acknowledgements

*W*e received a lot of help from many people and we want to thank them for their efforts in making the publication of this book possible. We especially appreciate Venerable Tzu Jung, the Chief Executive of Fo Guang Shan International Translation Center (F.G.S.I.T.C.), Venerable Hui Chuan, the Abbot of Hsi Lai Temple, and Venerable Yi Chao, the Director of F.G.S.I.T.C. for their support and leadership; Audrey Her, Kevin Tseng, Mae Chu, Madelon Wheeler-Gibb, Shujan Cheng, and Tom Manzo for their translation; Brenda Bolinger for her editing; Bill Maher, Echo Tsai, Mu-Tzen Hsu, Oscar Mauricio for their proofreading; Mei-Chi Shih for her book and cover design; Venerable Miao Han, for preparing the manuscript for publication. Our appreciation also goes to everyone who has supported this project from its conception to its completion.

Introduction to
the Sutra of the Medicine Buddha

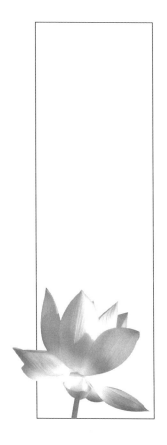

Introduction to
the Sutra of the Medicine Buddha

The "*Meritorious Virtues and Original Vows of the Medicine Buddha of Azure Radiance Sutra*" is often referred to in an abbreviated form, as the "*Sutra of the Meritorious Virtues of Medicine Buddha's Original Vows,*" the "*Sutra of the Meritorious Virtues of Medicine Buddha's Original Vows,*" or simply, the "*Sutra of the Medicine Buddha.*" The entire sutra is a single volume in total, translated into Chinese from the Sanskrit original by Venerable Master Xuanzang (596-664 C.E.) of the Tang Dynasty. Venerable Master Xuanzang was a native of Gou County, Luo State (now Yanshi, Honan Province). His lay name was Chen Yi. He was called "Tripitaka"[1] because he was an expert in the study of Sutra, Vinaya, and Abidharma. He was an outstanding sutra translator and the founder of the Mind-Only (*Faxiang*) School.[2] In 629 C.E., Xuanzang set off for India. Traveling alone, he encountered many hardships and dangers, and after his arrival, he remained in India for seventeen years of extensive study. In 648 C.E., he returned to Changan with 520 collections of teachings and 657 texts written in Sanskrit. Throughout his lifetime, he translated 75 sutras and commentaries (totaling 1,335 fascicles) into Chinese.

This particular sutra narrates how the Buddha, in response to Manjusri Bodhisattva's request, spoke to highly cultivated monastics, bodhisattvas, kings, and magistrates concerning the meritorious virtues of Medicine Buddha's Eastern Pure Land of Azure Radiance. A Pure Land, or Buddha Field, is the sphere of spiritual influence of one particular Buddha. The sphere of influence a Buddha presides over is determined by the vows that the Buddha has taken while still a bodhisattva. The following brief summary of the great vows that Medicine Buddha generated when he was a bodhisattva show us how he was able to eventually fashion his own Pure Land into a magnificent one, free of every cause of suffering and furnished with everything necessary for the happiness, well-being, and liberation of its inhabitants.

(1.) The first vow: May all sentient beings realize that they are the same as all Buddhas.

The Medicine Buddha's initial vow is that when he attains Buddhahood, not only will his body shine forth as a bright light illuminating innumerable worlds, but it will also be adorned with the thirty-two excellent marks and the eighty noble qualities of The True Man. In the meantime, he wishes that all sentient beings might have bodies like his because their Buddha Nature is shrouded by ignorance. Therefore, Medicine Buddha vows to remove the shroud of agitation and anxiety with his Buddha Light, thus helping them realize Buddhahood.

(2.) The second vow: May all sentient beings awaken and engage in beneficial actions.

The first vow is to show that Buddhas and all sentient beings are equal in the realm of Dharmakaya.[3] The second vow is to use Nirmanakaya,[4] the manifestation of Dharmakaya, to teach and benefit all sentient beings. Ordinary people's bodies also have the crystal radiance of Wisdom. However, this light cannot illuminate within and without due to agitation and anxiety. When Medicine Buddha sends forth light from his body, any sentient being that is caught in the depths of profound darkness and gloom can be illuminated and become awake. It is like the blind regaining their eyesight within the warm and tender light of the Buddha. Now that they can see, they can engage in all manner of activities which benefit both themselves and others. Therefore, Buddhas and bodhisattvas not only guide all sentient beings to cultivate their body and mind, they also teach them knowledge and skills which are mutually beneficial.

③ The third vow: May all sentient beings enjoy abundant resources.

Nowadays, skillful application of modern advanced technology makes it possible for people to enjoy the benefits of food, clothing, and transportation. However, if we do not recognize the immeasurable wisdom which is the ingenious foundation of all application, our application may be anything but skillful. Once people sense an imbalance in the resources they possess, greed, anger, and ignorance arise and one war follows another. Therefore, Medicine Buddha vows that all sentient beings shall have the light of wisdom, revealing to them no scarcity of nurturing resources, and these sentient beings shall be able to cease fighting among themselves, be at peace, and enjoy the abundance of food, clothing, etc.

④ The fourth vow: May all sentient beings abide on the path of the great vehicle.

The second and third vows focus on materialistic aspects of life, such as being engaged in beneficial activities and enjoying resources. The fourth vow focuses on the completion of correct view and correct understanding. Medicine Buddha vows that all sentient beings who are dwelling in the three lower realms, due to their disbelief concerning the law of causation and resultant bad effects, may take leave of the wayward path through listening to the teachings of the Buddha and engaging in the spiritual disciplines of precepts, meditative concentration, and wisdom. The vow also includes the wish that those who are proceeding in spiritual development via the sravaka or pratyeka-buddha[5] vehicle may become engaged by means of the great vehicle.

The first, second, third, and fourth vows are meant to bestow all sentient beings with joy. The fifth through twelfth vows can be generalized as those concerning the elimination of suffering in its multiple facets. All twelve vows were practiced by the Medicine Buddha while he was still a bodhisattva. What kind of Pure Land was a bodhisattva eventually able to fashion through the strength of those vows? The Pure Land of the Medicine Buddha is described as a pristine land of Crystal Radiance, a world of abundance. All sentient beings in this land or field of affluence have no economic worries because there are abundant resources. The accessibility of food, clothing, housing, and transportation is of great convenience and entertainment is available according to one's wishes. Since the sentient beings of that Pure Land are inspired by Medicine Buddha to cultivate their spiritual practice, all kinds of blessings and virtuous causes and conditions are brought forth from the benevolent karma they previously created. Should they desire to become business entrepreneurs, they will have no need to worry about long delays in requisitions or about operating at a loss. Should they desire to design products that benefit others, they will experience no anxiety due to lack of materials or heavy taxes.

The second facet of the Pure Land is that it is a pristine, unblemished society. The society that we are living in right now is compromised by harmful views, thoughts, and desires and is filled with frustration and anxiety. The pristine land of Crystal Radiance is a society where all of its members remain uncorrupted. Since there are neither male nor female forms[6] in this Pure Land, the society is free from all the suffering connected with infidelity. Since there are no beings of the lower realms present, there is no hell and no ferocious beasts or hungry ghosts. In the pristine land of Crystal Radiance there are no

4

social problems such as fighting, killing, or addictions of any kind.

Thirdly, it is a world of enlightened functioning politics. In the pristine land of Crystal Radiance, there is no criminal punishment, jail, torture, or corrupt officials.

Fourthly, this Pure Land is a world of perfect health and joyful living. In this Pure Land, every sentient being is physically and mentally healthy and enjoys life abundantly. Not only do sentient beings not suffer from any illness, they also do not experience any anxiety or frustration due to greed, anger, and jealously. The sentient beings in this Pure Land usually aid others in seeking liberation.

These sentient beings not only enjoy abundant resources and live in peace and joy, they also receive teachings from Medicine Buddha. The essence of the sutra is concerned with the skillful ways the Medicine Buddha teaches and the benefits his teaching brings the sentient beings of this Pure Land. These teachings and their benefits can be briefly described as follows:

— Recollecting and contemplating the virtues seeded within the Medicine Buddha's titles can remove four kinds of obstructions and deliver four kinds of benefits. The four kinds of obstructions are greed and stinginess; fault finding and arrogance; jealousy, cursing, and slander; and engagement in argument and litigation. The four kinds of benefits are the benefits of birth in this Pure Land, birth in the heavenly realm, birth in the human realm, and birth in the human form capable of becoming a great person.

— A sentient being's illnesses and suffering can be uprooted by reciting the Medicine Buddha's Mantra.

— Making offerings and prostrations to Medicine Buddha can garner protection from Manjusri Bodhisattva and the protectors of the heavenly realm. By engaged practice of the Dharma of

Medicine Buddha, all sentient beings can receive four particularly beneficial outcomes: longevity, wealth, high occupational positions, and a male or female offspring according to the parents' wishes. Moreover, the arising of various strange phenomena as well as all varieties of fear will subside. All calamities due to warfare, declining morality, all forms of violation, and the risks associated with childbirth will be eliminated.

May this sutra, with its emphasis on releasing sentient beings' suffering and bestowing joy in this present life, serve as a precious Dharma solution for the practical issues in life.

Notes

1 Tripitaka: Buddhist canon. The Buddha's teachings form a canon known as the Tripitaka, or "three baskets," because they were divided into three categories: the Sutra (teachings of the Buddha); the Vinaya (precepts and rules); and the Abidharma (commentaries on the Buddha's teachings). There are two major sets of Tripitaka or canon: the Theravada canon written in Pali, and the Mahayana canon written in Sanskrit and preserved in Chinese and Tibetan. The Mahayana canon includes all the texts of the Theravada canon in addition to its own sutras and commentaries.

2 The Mind-Only (Faxiang) School: is one of the eight major schools of Buddhism and was established in China upon the return of Xuanzang, consequent on his translation of the Mind-Only works. Its aim is to understand the principle underlying the myriad phenomena or nature and characteristic of all things.

3 Dharmakaya: The Buddha's Body of Truth, which is empty in and of itself.

4 Nirmanakaya: The transformation of the body of Buddha, the Body-of-Form of all Buddhas which is manifested for the sake of beings who cannot yet approach the Dharmakaya, the formless True Body of Buddhahood.

5 sravaka: Literally, the word "sravaka" means hearer, and it refers to one who has attained enlightenment after listening to the Buddha's teachings; "pratyeka-buddha" refers to one who awakens to the Truth through their own efforts when they live in the time without a Buddha's presence. Sravakas and pratyeka-buddhas seek enlightenment only for themselves, in contrast to bodhisattvas who seek liberation for all beings.

6 female forms: The sutra mentions the absence of female forms only, but since "male" forms cannot exist without the existence of the conceptual counterpart "female", it is fair to say that neither "male" nor "female," as particular categories, exist in this Pure Land.

Sutra of
the Medicine Buddha

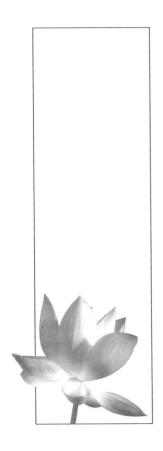

Incense Offering

Incense burning in the censer,
all space permeated with fragrance.

Buddhas perceive it from every direction.
Auspicious clouds gather everywhere.

With our sincerity,
Buddhas manifest themselves in their
entirety.

We take refuge in the bodhisattvas,
mahasattvas.

Sutra of the Medicine Buddha[1]

Thus, I have heard[2]:

One time,[3] while traveling and teaching throughout several countries, the Bhagavan[4] arrived at the magnificent city Vaisali.[5] There he sat beneath the Joyful Tree of Musical Breezes[6] and was joined by a great multitude of beings, both human and non-human. In attendance was a retinue of highly cultivated bhiksus,[7] eight thousand in number. Accompanying them was a throng of bodhisattvas[8] and great bodhisattvas,[9] thirty-six thousand in total. Also in attendance were kings and their subjects, brahmins,[10] laity, and a constellation of celestial beings.[11] This great congregation respectfully gathered around the Buddha to hear his teaching.

At that time, the Dharma Prince Manjusri,[12] with inspired awareness of the Buddha's great power to influence, arose from his seat and came before the Buddha. Baring his right shoulder and bowing upon his right knee with joined palms,[13] the young prince implored, "World-Honored One,[14] we wish that you would speak to us about the various Buddhas' names and honorary titles, their great vows, and their magnificent virtues. We hope that all who are within hearing of these words can become free of karmic obstructions. Moreover, for the sake of sentient beings[15] in the Period of Semblance Dharma,[16] we hope these beneficial words can make them truly happy."

Upon hearing this request, the World-Honored One praised Manjusri. "Excellent, excellent, Manjusri! It is out of your deep and heartfelt compassion for sentient beings that you have implored me to speak of the Buddhas' names and titles, original vows, and virtues that accompany them. This is in order to release sentient beings' entanglements in karmic obstructions and also to bring peace and joy to those of the Period of Semblance Dharma. Now, for your benefit, I am going to speak. You should listen attentively and contemplate carefully what I am going to say." "Splendid!" replied Manjusri. "We are most happy to hear from you."

Buddha thus began to speak, "Manjusri, east of here beyond Buddha lands as innumerable as the sands of Ganges Rivers, there exists a Buddha world called 'The Land of Pure Crystal'[17] where 'Medicine Buddha of Pure Crystal Radiance'[18] presides. Adorned with sacred titles, this Buddha is commonly honored as, 'Worthy of Offerings,'[19] 'Absolute Universal Enlightened Awareness,'[20] 'Activity of Bright Fullness,'[21] 'Immaculately Departed One,'[22] 'Transcendent Understanding of the Ordinary World,'[23] 'Unexcelled One,'[24] 'The True Man Who Tames and Harmonizes,'[25] 'Teacher of Divine and Human Beings,'[26] 'Awakened One,'[27] and 'Bhagavan.'

Manjusri, twelve great vows evolved from the heart of the World-Honored Medicine Buddha of Pure Crystal Radiance as he advanced upon the bodhisattva path. These vows were made with the heartfelt wish that all sentient beings might fulfill their aspirations.

The first vow is this: 'In a future lifetime, may I attain Anuttara-Samyak-Sambodhi.[28] Thus, my body shall be one of bright radiance, shining forth in blazing illumination, without measure, boundary, or limitation, lighting up innumerable worlds. This body will be adorned with the thirty-two marks of excellence[29] and the eighty noble qualities,[30] which accompany the form of The True Man. May all sentient beings become illuminated and recognize this body of bright radiance as their own.'

The second vow is this: 'In a future lifetime, upon my

enlightenment, may my body be of the clarity of pure crystal, within and without, flawless and impeccable. May it be of boundless radiance and majestic virtue, of serene abiding goodness. May this body be a magnificent incendiary net of glory,[31] more brilliant than sun and moon, able to embrace and awaken even those beings caught in the depths of profound darkness and gloom. Thus, shall all beings accomplish their endeavors according to their intentions.'

The third vow is this: 'In a future lifetime, upon my enlightenment, may I enable all beings to gain an abundance of things most useful and enjoyable, eliminating all scarcity or want. This I will accomplish through boundless wisdom and skillful means[32] beyond measure.'

The fourth vow is this: 'In a future lifetime, upon my enlightenment, may all sentient beings choose to follow the peaceful way of bodhi,[33] instead of traveling the path of evil practices. If there are beings who are proceeding via the sravaka or pratyeka-buddha[34] vehicle, may they become engaged by means of the great vehicle.'[35]

The fifth vow is this: 'In a future lifetime, upon my enlightenment, may sentient beings beyond number practice wholesome living and uphold all precepts according to my teachings. Through the commitment to actualize the Dharma, may they accomplish the Tri-Vidhani Silani.[36] When beings violate any precept, their purity can be restored and they can avoid falling into the suffering realms simply upon hearing my name.'

The sixth vow is this: 'In a future lifetime, upon my enlightenment, I vow to aid all sentient beings who suffer any form of malady. I vow to relieve those whose bodies are deformed, who are without complete sense faculties, who lack beauty and appeal, or who are simple-minded or foolishly stubborn. Those who are blind, deaf, raspy-voiced, or mute, who suffer with palsied or crippled limbs, who are hunchbacks or lepers or insane, or who encounter any other form of infirmity; all these shall, after hearing my name, gain optimum health and intuitive mastery of all knowledge and skills. They shall find themselves in complete possession of all faculties and no longer experience the suffering of illness.'

The seventh vow is this: 'In a future lifetime, upon my enlightenment, if there are any sentient beings who are tormented by illness, who have no hope of release or respite from their suffering, who are without doctors or medicine, or who have no family members or other caregivers to assist them, who are homeless or impoverished, or are suffering in any way, I vow that once the sounding of my name has penetrated their ears, all illness shall cease, and they shall find serene contentment in body and mind. They shall be surrounded by family and caregivers and all that they have previously lacked shall become abundantly available to them, even unto the actualization of Buddhahood.'

The eighth vow is this: 'In a future lifetime, upon my enlightenment, if there are any women who feel coerced or oppressed by the many disadvantages of the female form[37] and have generated the desire to let go of that form, they shall, after hearing my name be transformed into the male form. Accompanying this form are all these characteristics of the true man, even unto the attainment of Buddhahood.'

The ninth vow is this: 'In a future lifetime, upon my enlightenment, all who are caught in the net of evil shall be released from their entanglement in heterodox practices.[38] If there are those who have fallen into the dark forest of evil views, they shall all become established in the correct perspective and gradually assume all the bodhisattvas' disciplines,[39] quickly actualizing Buddhahood.' *2 L QUESTIONABLE? Future*

The tenth vow is this: 'In a future lifetime, upon my enlightenment, if there are any sentient beings who, due to the enforcement of local laws, find themselves sentenced to flogging, incarceration, torture, execution, or any other manner of brutal punishment, they shall be aided by hearing my name. For those who are insulted, humiliated, or in abject misery or who are oppressed by burning anxiety, suffering in both body and mind, if they hear my name, due to the power of my awe-inspiring spiritual elan,[40] all shall gain release from their suffering and woes.'

The eleventh vow is this: 'In a future lifetime, upon my enlightenment, if there are any sentient beings who commit wrongdoings due to the agony of hunger and thirst, they shall be aided by hearing my name and concentrating on it. First, by providing exquisite delicacies, I will bring about their complete bodily satisfaction and contentment. Physically sated, they may then enjoy the wondrous flavor of the Dharma and become established in spiritual satisfaction and contentment.'

The twelfth vow is this: 'In a future lifetime, upon my enlightenment, if there are any sentient beings who are without clothing due to poverty, who day and night suffer the afflictions of extreme heat and cold and the torment of insects, they shall be aided by hearing my name and concentrating on it. They shall instantly be afforded that which they wish: the acquisition of many kinds of exquisite clothing, precious gems as adornment, flowered hair ornaments, perfumed ointments, and musical entertainment. The full enjoyment of all these things shall evoke their complete satisfaction and contentment.

Manjusri, these are the twelve supremely subtle and

"CONTENTMENT"

wonderful vows of the 'World-Honored Medicine Buddha of Pure Crystal Radiance, Worthy of Offerings, Absolute Universal Enlightened Awareness' while he was practicing the bodhisattva path."

Again the Buddha said to Manjusri, "Even in one or more kalpas,[41] I could not finish speaking of the magnificent vows the Medicine Buddha pledged while on the bodhisattva path, nor fully describe the wonders of the pristine Buddha land he attained. I can tell you this Buddha land is infinitely pure. There are no women's forms,[42] nor lower forms of rebirth, nor sound of suffering. The land itself is made of pure crystal with ropes of gold outlining the paths. There are magnificent palaces and pavilions with spacious windows strung with nets, all made of the seven precious gems. The virtue and magnificence of this Buddha land is no different from that of the Western Pure Land.[43] In this Buddha realm, among the innumerable bodhisattvas, there are two bodhisattvas at the highest level, preceding Buddhahood. Their names are Radiant Sunlight Bodhisattva[44] and Radiant Moonlight Bodhisattva.[45] Both bodhisattvas are skillful in upholding the Medicine Buddha's Dharma. Thus, Manjusri, all good men and good women who have confidence and faith should vow to be born in this Buddha land."

Continuing in this manner, the World-Honored One said to Manjusri, "There are sentient beings who do not know the difference between beneficial and harmful conduct. Bent on acquiring and maintaining advantages for themselves alone, they remain greedy and closefisted, unaware of the beneficial fruit of giving. Ignorant and therefore lacking in any trust in the merit of giving, they desperately accumulate and guard their material riches. Thus, upon meeting a beggar, they experience suffering from the knowledge that they will receive nothing in return for their donation. So strong is their attachment to their riches that to part with even a portion of them is like parting with a portion of their own flesh.

Manjusri, there are innumerable sentient beings, who being stingy and greedy, amass great resources and wealth. Yet, they are incapable of enjoying that which they have accumulated for themselves, let alone sharing any of their wealth with their parents, spouses, stewards, servants, or beggars. Those sentient beings who die in this frame of mind will be reborn in either the hungry ghost or animal realm. However, due to the fact that while in the human realm, they temporarily had the chance to hear the name of the Medicine Buddha, upon remembering this Buddha's name they shall immediately be reborn in the human realm. Influenced by the memory of that past-life experience and suffering of the lower realms, they are willing to forego the enjoyment of sensual pleasures and enter into activities of generosity as well as praising the efforts of anyone who gives. They are no longer attached to their possessions, and are gradually even willing to share portions of their bodies, if necessary, with any who request, let alone the remainder of their wealth and possessions.

And Manjusri, there are sentient beings who still break the precepts even though they have received the Buddha's teachings concerning them. Also, there are those who do not break the precepts per se, but they do, however, break rules and regulations pertaining to daily life. Then there are those who are successful in keeping the precepts and adhering to the rules and regulations of daily life, but they do not have the right view. Subsequently, those who have the right view, but waste or avoid the opportunity to further their learning, cannot encounter the deep and profound meaning of the Buddha's teachings. Then there are those who pursue opportunities to learn, but do so with an arrogant attitude. This conceit prevents them from acquiring any knowledge, but they still consider themselves as right, and others as wrong. This mindset leads them to criticize the Dharma and undermines their understanding of the truth. As they ignorantly and incorrectly practice the Dharma, they harmfully influence others, causing them to fall into a dangerous pit. All these beings shall find themselves endlessly migrating in the lower realms.

However, if these beings are able to hear the name of the Medicine Buddha of Pure Crystal Radiance, they can thereupon give up harmful practices and undertake all beneficial ones, no longer entering any lower realms. There are some who cannot abandon their unwholesome practices right away, and they will drop into the lower realms. Here, through the power of the Buddha's vows, when they eventually hear the Buddha's name chanted even for a moment, their existence in the lower realms is concluded, and they will be reborn in the human realm. Then they will gain right view and right diligence and properly attain the mind of joy. Thereupon, they are able to give up conventional living to initiate monastic life. They are capable of receiving and upholding the precepts without violation. By taking advantage of opportunities to hear the Dharma with the right view, they become capable of understanding it on a deep and profound level. No longer ignorantly and incorrectly practicing the Dharma, they gradually develop bodhisattva characteristics and quickly gain all-embracing completeness.

Manjusri, if there are sentient beings who are stingy, greedy, jealous, boasting of self and slandering of others, they will fall into the three lower realms for innumerable thousands of years. After they have endured severe pain and suffering there, they are born once again in the human realm, but as cows, horses, camels, or donkeys. These animals must bear heavy loads and walk long distances. Constantly subjected to whippings, thirst, and hunger, they are driven to exhaustion and anguish. Or, such beings are born as human, but in very lowly despicable states. As the servants and slaves of people, they are constantly commanded to labor for others with no freedom for themselves.

If, however, in former lives in the human realm, they have heard the name of the Medicine Buddha of Pure Crystal Radiance and are able to remember it, they can wholeheartedly take refuge in the Buddha. Because of the strength of this Buddha's unique spiritual elan, they are liberated from all their sufferings. All their faculties are keen, and they are wise and learned, constantly seeking the superlative Dharma. They are able to meet beneficial friends who encourage their development of virtue. They forever cut the net of entanglements, break through the shell of ignorance, and cease the river of deluded thoughts. They are set free from the worry, suffering, and agitation that accompany birth, old age, illness, and death.

Again, Manjusri, if there are sentient beings who are habitually contrary and divisive, who engage in mutual fighting and litigation, aggravating and disturbing both self and others by means of body, speech, and mind, these beings increase the occurrence of malevolent deeds. They call upon the spirits that reside in mountains, forest, trees, or tombs, such as yaksas or raksasas.[46] As an act of worship, they slay a sentient being and offer up its blood and flesh. Then they write the name of the person they hold a grudge against and make an image in their likeness, using the technique of wizardry to cast a curse upon it.

ous precious multi-colored blossoms, where each is instantly reborn in the center of the blooms.

Or, if the resolve of these beings is weaker yet, they will be reborn in one of the heavenly realms. Despite this rebirth, their good roots remain intact. Therefore, after their life span in the heavenly realms, they will not be reborn in any of the lower realms, but instead, return to be born in the human realm. There they may be born as a cakravartin,[55] a world sovereign of great virtue who effortlessly unites the four continents,[56] peacefully establishing unlimited sentient beings in the ten good ways.[57] Or, they may be born as a kasatriya,[58] brahmin, or a member of a prominent, prosperous family with numerous relatives, with overflowing abundance of wealth and material possessions. They have a pleasing appearance, and are astute, wise, courageous, and valiant, possessing physical health, strength, and energy. Or, if they were previously women, and were able to hear the name of the Medicine Buddha of Pure Crystal Radiance and wholeheartedly receive and uphold it, they will not again receive a woman's form.

Manjusri, at the time of his enlightenment and due to the strength of his original vows, the Medicine Buddha of Pure Crystal Radiance was capable of seeing numerous sentient beings encountering various forms of illness, such as emaciation, yellow fever, and disorientation due to magical practices. He also observed them suffering due to premature demise, or an unexpected or violent death.

Wanting to relieve these beings' suffering and illness, to fulfill all that they seek, he then, at that moment, entered into the samadhi[59] called 'Eliminating the Suffering and Agitation of all Beings.' Upon entering meditative absorption, a great light emanated from the crown of the Buddha's head. Immersed in ous precious multi-colored blossoms, where each is instantly reborn in the center of the blooms.

Or, if the resolve of these beings is weaker yet, they will be reborn in one of the heavenly realms. Despite this rebirth, their good roots remain intact. Therefore, after their life span in the heavenly realms, they will not be reborn in any of the lower realms, but instead, return to be born in the human realm. There they may be born as a cakravartin,[55] a world sovereign of great virtue who effortlessly unites the four continents,[56] peacefully establishing unlimited sentient beings in the ten good ways.[57] Or, they may be born as a kasatriya,[58] brahmin, or a member of a prominent, prosperous family with numerous relatives, with overflowing abundance of wealth and material possessions. They have a pleasing appearance, and are astute, wise, courageous, and valiant, possessing physical health, strength, and energy. Or, if they were previously women, and were able to hear the name of the Medicine Buddha of Pure Crystal Radiance and wholeheartedly receive and uphold it, they will not again receive a woman's form.

Manjusri, at the time of his enlightenment and due to the strength of his original vows, the Medicine Buddha of Pure Crystal Radiance was capable of seeing numerous sentient beings encountering various forms of illness, such as emaciation, yellow fever, and disorientation due to magical practices. He also observed them suffering due to premature demise, or an unexpected or violent death.

Wanting to relieve these beings' suffering and illness, to fulfill all that they seek, he then, at that moment, entered into the samadhi[59] called 'Eliminating the Suffering and Agitation of all Beings.' Upon entering meditative absorption, a great light emanated from the crown of the Buddha's head. Immersed in this light, the Buddha then recited a great dharani:[60]

'Namas[61] Bhagavat Bhaisajyaguru Vaidurya Prabha Raja Tathagata[62] Arhat[63] Samyaksambuddha[64] Tadyatha Om[65] Bhaisajya[66] Bhaishgajye Bhaishajya Samudgate Savha.'[67]

Having uttered the dharani in the midst of such great light, the earth began trembling and sent forth a great radiance. All sentient beings' illness and suffering were healed and they enjoyed total ease of body and mind.

Manjusri, if you see men and women who suffer from illness you should, with a devoted heart and mind, help bathe them, cleanse their mouths, and administer food or medicine or water which has been purified through one hundred and eight recitations of the dharani. All their illness and suffering shall thereupon be extinguished. If there is something they wish for, simply by reciting the Dharma wholeheartedly, they shall obtain it. Thus, they shall enjoy a long life free from illness. After their life has come to an end, they shall be reborn in the realm of the Medicine Buddha, where, without any regression, they advance to supreme enlightenment.

Manjusri, there are men and women who wholehearted-ly, earnestly, and respectfully make offerings to the Medicine Buddha of Pure Crystal Radiance and who often uphold this dharani without neglect, never forgetting it. Also, Manjusri, there are men and women of pure faith who have the chance to hear and recite all the titles of the Medicine Buddha of Pure Crystal Radiance who chew on the teeth-cleansing twig,[68] rinse the mouth, and bathe the body before they offer fragrant flowers and incense and various kinds of devotional music to the image of the Medicine Buddha. Then there are those who record or copy the sutra or teach others to transcribe it, and who listen to the sutra and understand its meaning, thereupon wholeheartedly upholding it. If there is a monastic who specializes in teaching the practice of the Medicine Buddha, one should offer all that is necessary for daily living, ensuring that the teacher lacks nothing. All of these mentioned will thereupon be protected and will be in the awareness of all Buddhas; that which they wish for will be fulfilled on their path to enlightenment."

At that time, Manjusri spoke to the Buddha, "World-Honored One, I will vow, at the time of the Period of Semblance Dharma, with various skillful means, to make it possible for all good men and good women of pure faith to hear the titles of the World-Honored Medicine Buddha of Pure Crystal Radiance. Even while asleep they are able to awaken to truth through hearing this sound in their ear.

I will also make possible the upholding of this sutra through various skillful means such as recitation, explication of its profound meaning, self-practice through transcribing, or teaching others to transcribe it. Other means also include respectfully making offerings to the sutra itself by cleaning and purifying the environment and preparing an elevated place as an altar upon which the sutra is placed. Having made mottled silk bags of the five colors, and placing the sutra therein, offerings can be made of the various fragrances of flowers, pastes, powders, and incense along with garlands of precious gems and jade, parasols, banners, and devotional music. Upon the completion of these offerings, the Four Heavenly Kings[69] and their retinue of hundreds of thousands of heavenly beings shall arrive at that place and offer their protection.

World-Honored One, wherever this precious sutra is introduced, due to the virtue of the original vows of the Medicine Buddha of Pure Crystal Radiance, the hearing of his titles, and the upholding of this sutra, that place shall be free from the occurrence of any violent deaths. Those living in this area shall be protected from the seizure of their vital energy by ghosts. For those who have been deprived of their vital energy in this manner, they shall have it returned to them and enjoy peace of body and mind."

The Buddha then responded to Manjusri, "Yes! Yes! It is as you have said, Manjusri. If there are men and women of pure practice who desire to make offerings to the World-Honored Medicine Buddha of Pure Crystal Radiance, they ought to, first, set up an image of the Buddha in a clean and peaceful place, surrounding it with various flowers, fragrant burning incense, and colorful streamers and banners.

For seven days and nights, they should uphold the eight precepts, eat vegetarian meals, bathe the body to become clean and fragrant, and don clean clothing. With a mind free from turbidity, anger, and the desire to harm, they should give rise to a beneficial mind of peace, loving-kindness, compassion, joy, equanimity,[70] and equality for all sentient beings. They should circle the Buddha statue in a clockwise direction, drumming and singing songs of joyous praise. They should also contemplate the Buddha's vows of great virtue, study and recite this sutra, consider its meanings, and speak to reveal the profound teaching. If these pure practices are followed, all their wishes shall be granted. Those who seek long life shall gain long life. All who seek abundant wealth shall gain abundant wealth. Those who seek a government post shall receive such. All those who seek the birth of a male child or the birth of a female child shall be granted such.

If there is anyone who unexpectedly experiences nightmares, apparitions, the ominous gathering of strange birds, or the arising of various strange phenomena around their residence, should he or she make offerings of numerous exquisite material objects, all these omens shall disappear without doing any harm. If there are those who encounter fears due to flood, fire, calamities of warfare, near death experiences, or vicious wild animals such as elephants, lions, tigers, wolves, brown bears, poisonous snakes, scorpions, centipedes, millipedes, mosquitoes, and biting flies, when they can wholeheartedly contemplate the Buddha and respectfully make offerings to him, all their fears shall subside. If they have fears due to being invaded by other countries or because of internal rebellions or the activities of robbers and thieves, upon respectfully contemplating the Buddha, they shall find relief from these fears.

Again Manjusri, suppose there are good men and good women of pure faith who, even unto death, have not followed the path of any other faith and take refuge in the Buddha, the Dharma, and the Sangha and uphold the various sets of precepts, such as the five precepts,[71] the ten precepts,[72] the four hundred bodhisattva precepts, the two hundred and fifty bhiksu precepts, and the five hundred bhiksuni precepts. If, in the midst of upholding these precepts they violate any of them and thus become fearful of falling into the three lower realms upon rebirth,[73] should they become absorbed in the contemplation of the Buddha's titles and respectfully make offerings, they can be certain of no further rebirth in these realms.

When an expectant mother is experiencing the pains of labor, by chanting the Buddha's name as an offering, all of her fears and apprehension shall be removed. Due to the smooth delivery, the form and five faculties of the baby shall be perfectly complete. His or her countenance shall be very pleasant, such that people will be delighted when they see the baby. This child shall be inherently astute, enjoy a peaceful existence, and encounter little illness. No non-human being shall be capable of seizing that child's vital energy."

At that time, the World-Honored One spoke to Ananda[74] saying, "Thus I acknowledge all the virtues of the World-Honored Medicine Buddha of Pure Crystal Radiance. This virtuous state is shared by all Buddhas as a result of their deep and profound practice, but it is very difficult for ordinary people to understand. How about you, Ananda, do you trust this?" Ananda replied, "World-Honored One, with regard to the sutra spoken by the Buddha, I have absolutely no doubts concerning it. Why is that so? Because all the activities proceeding from the Buddha's body, speech, and mind are already completely pure. Even though the sun and moon may fall from the sky, even though the tallest mountain may collapse, the words of every Buddha are not subject to change. World-Honored One, there are many beings who are not equipped with the roots of faith. Upon hearing the discussion of the profound state shared by all Buddhas, these beings question why would such various remarkable benefits accrue to one who simply contemplates and recites the titles of the Medicine Buddha of Pure Crystal Radiance. Due to this lack of trust, they even go so far as to engage in slander. As a result, they remain in the endless darkness of ignorance, thus losing the opportunity for great benefit and happiness, and repeatedly falling into various lower realms."

The Buddha thus spoke to Ananda, "For those particular sentient beings, if they hear the titles of the World-Honored Medicine Buddha of Pure Crystal Radiance and uphold them without doubt and bewilderment, there is no point in even being concerned about falling into lower realms of rebirth. Ananda, this is the deep and profound practice of all Buddhas, found difficult to believe and understand by most. Your comprehension of this can be ascribed to the power of the Buddha's practices as well, Ananda. All sravakas, pratyeka-buddhas, and bodhisattvas who have not yet ascended the first of the ten stages of bodhisattva development,[75] are not yet able to understand and know the true nature of this practice. Only those bodhisattvas who will attain Buddhahood in their next lifetime[76] are capable of true understanding. Ananda, it is difficult to be reborn in human form. Having faith in the Triple Gem[77] is also not easy. Most difficult to achieve, however, is the opportunity to hear the titles of the World-Honored Medicine Buddha of Pure Crystal Radiance. Ananda, the Medicine Buddha of Pure Crystal Radiance has practiced unlimited bodhisattva spiritual disciplines, as well as developed innumerable wonderful skillful means and achieved numerous great vows. Were I to elaborate on this Buddha's disciplines, skillful means, and vows, for one kalpa or more, I could not describe them completely for they are vast and limitless."

Subsequently, a great bodhisattva named Rescuing Aid Bodhisattva[78] arose from the audience. With bared right shoulder, and bowing upon his right knee with joined palms, he respectfully spoke to the Buddha saying, "Great Virtuous World-Honored One, during the Period of Semblance Dharma, there will be many sentient beings who will be trapped by various kinds of suffering and adversity. They will experience long periods of illness and grow weak and feeble. Unable to eat and drink, their lips and throats will become parched and dry. No matter where they look, they shall see only darkness, and exhibit all the symptoms of approaching death. Their mothers, fathers, relatives, and friends will gather around them, weeping and wailing. However, unaware of their concern, those on their deathbeds will be experiencing the arrival of the Judgment King of Hell's[79] messenger who escorts their consciousness' into the presence of the King. Subsequently, these beings clearly recollecting all their deeds, both good and bad, record them and deliver their lists of deeds to the Judgment King of Hell. Thereafter, that King will interrogate them, and after considering the number of deeds, both good and bad, will deliver an appropriate decision concerning their lives. If, at that time, the parents, relatives, and friends of those who are sick take refuge in the World-Honored Medicine Buddha of Pure Crystal Radiance, request many monastics to recite this sutra, light seven layers of lamps,[80] display the five-colored longevity banners,[81] or undertake any similar practices on their behalf, their consciousness' can return after seven, twenty one, thirty-five, or forty-nine days.[82] When their consciousness' return, it is like waking up from a dream. Through this experience, they remember all their good and bad deeds as well as the karmic retribution, thus proving to themselves the connection between cause and effect. Hereafter, they no longer are engaged in activities that create bad karma. Therefore, all good men and good women of pure faith should receive and uphold the titles of the Medicine Buddha of Pure Crystal Radiance, and according to their ability, respectfully make offerings to him."

At that time, Ananda asked Rescuing Aid Bodhisattva, "How should one make offerings to the Buddha? Furthermore, concerning the longevity banners and lamps, how should one engage in this type of activity?" Rescuing Aid Bodhisattva then spoke, "Great Virtuous One,[83] if there are sick people who seek relief from their suffering, those who care about them can, on their behalf, uphold the eight precepts for seven days and nights. According to their means, they can make offerings of food, drink, and material possessions to monastics. Throughout the day, they can bow and make offerings before the World-Honored Medicine Buddha of Pure Crystal Radiance, recite this sutra forty-nine times, and light forty-nine lamps. They can create seven images of the Buddha and place seven lamps in front of each. The glow from each lamp should be as large as the circumference of a wheel, and the radiant brightness should never be extinguished during the forty-nine days. Assemble the splendid five-colored longevity banners, each of which is composed of forty-nine three-finger-length sections.[84] Also, they can set free forty-nine living beings of various kinds. Due to this activity, the sick individuals are supported in overcoming danger and distress, and are immune to being held hostage by any evil spirit.

Again, Ananda, if in a country, calamities arise such as epidemics, invasions, internal rebellions, strange changes in constellations, solar and lunar eclipses, untimely wind and rain, and drought, the ruler of that country should give rise to the heart and mind of compassion for all sentient beings, and grant amnesty to all who are imprisoned. In reference to what I have previously suggested concerning offerings, they also can, on behalf of all sentient beings, make offerings to the World-Honored Medicine Buddha of Pure Crystal Radiance. Because of these good roots and the strength of the Buddha's original vows, that country is able to quickly attain peace and stability. The wind and rain will arrive according to season and the harvest will be bountiful. All sentient beings will be free from illness and experience happiness. In the midst of this country there will be no harm or violence. Yaksas, demons, and other spirits that harass sentient beings and all evil phenomena will instantly disappear. Because the ruler engages in these activities on behalf of the populace, he shall remain energetic and enjoy a long life free from illness, in perfect ease.

Ananda, if the king, queen, the king's consorts, the prince, high ranking officials, prime ministers, palace servants, numerous officials, and the general public become troubled by illness or other difficulties, these people should assemble the five-colored longevity banners and light the lamps of continuous illumination. They also should set free various sentient beings, scatter multi-colored flowers, and light numerous types of incense. Thereafter, they shall recover from the illness they have suffered and be released from their many difficulties."

At that time, Ananda asked Rescuing Aid Bodhisattva, "Good Man, how is it that a life that is now at its end can still be lengthened and benefited by these various practices?"

Rescuing Aid Bodhisattva Replied, "Great Virtuous One, haven't you ever heard about the nine kinds of unfortunate death that the Buddha has spoken about? It is because of this that I encourage the assembling of longevity banners, lighting of lamps, and the cultivation of various blessings and virtues so that one does not have to experience suffering throughout one's life."

Ananda then asked, "What are the nine kinds of unfortunate death?"

Rescuing Aid Bodhisattva responded, "Say, for example, there are sentient beings who are suffering minor illnesses and find themselves without a doctor, medicine, or caregiver. Even though they might eventually find a doctor, they are administered the wrong medicine. Because it is a minor illness, they are not expected to die, but unfortunately, they do.

Some of these beings believe in harmful heterodoxical and magical practices, seeking evil teachers who presumptuously predict disaster or good fortune. Thereupon their lives become unstable and fearful and their hearts and minds are turned in the wrong direction. Unsure of themselves, they seek methods of divination to predict disasters and they kill various sentient beings as sacrifices in order to ask for blessings and protection from the deities and spirits of mountains and rivers. Although they hope to extend the duration of their life, eventually it is clear they cannot do so. Due to their foolishness and confusion, they believe in inverted evil points of view and subsequently suffer an unfortunate death. They are then reborn in hell without hope for release. This is what is referred to as the first unfortunate death.

The second kind of unfortunate death is execution due to the existing laws of a particular country. The third kind of unfortunate death comes about because of an indulgent lifestyle which consists of hunting for pleasure, carousing, drinking, and engaging in lewd and licentious behavior. Due to their limitless idleness, their death comes about through the snatching of their vital energy by non-human beings. The fourth kind of unfortunate death is burning to death. The fifth kind of unfortunate death is drowning. The sixth kind of unfortunate death is being devoured by vicious beasts. The seventh kind of unfortunate death is plummeting off a mountain cliff. The eighth kind of unfortunate death is caused by poison, a curse, or a living corpse. The ninth kind of unfortunate death is caused by severe hunger without relief. These are the unfortunate deaths that the Buddha briefly spoke about. Here we have mentioned nine kinds, but there are numerous other kinds as well. It would be difficult for me to mention them all.

Again, Ananda, the Judgment King of Hell is primarily in charge of the record book of both good and evil deeds. If there are sentient beings who do not respect their parents, or who commit one of the five violations,[85] or who damage or slander the Triple Gem, or who break the laws of their country, or violate the five precepts, the Judgment King of Hell will weigh and evaluate their deeds and punish them accordingly. This is the reason I now encourage all sentient beings to light lamps and assemble longevity banners and cultivate merit by the practice of releasing captive beings so that they might pass through suffering and stress without difficulties."

At that time, in the midst of the gathering, there were twelve Yaksas Generals who had been in attendance during the entire assembly. Their names were:

General Kumbhira;	General Vajra;
General Mihira;	General Andira;
General Anila;	General Shandira;
General Indra;	General Pajra;
General Sgrahdsin;	General Sindura;
General Catura;	General Vikarala

These twelve Yaksas Generals, each with their seven thousand-member retinue, raised their voices in praise to the Buddha, saying, "At last! Due to the blessings of the Buddha's omniscient power we now can hear the titles of the World-Honored Medicine Buddha of Pure Crystal Radiance and no longer need to experience the fears of the three lower realms. We, in one accord, wholeheartedly take refuge in the Buddha, the Dharma, and the Sangha for the duration of our lives in this form. We vow to bear responsibility for all sentient beings and to work towards their benefit. Because of this, there will be abundant peace and joy. We shall become the protectors of any village, town, city, country, or forest, which has been introduced to this sutra as well as their inhabitants who uphold the titles of the Medicine Buddha of Pure Crystal Radiance and make respectful offerings thereto. All shall find relief from their suffering and woes, and all existing wishes shall be fulfilled. If there are those who are seeking relief from an illness or a particular stressful situation, they should just recite this sutra. Using the five-colored ribbon streamers, they should tie a knot for each of our names. After their wishes are fulfilled, they can untie the knots."

At that time, the World-Honored One praised the Yaksas Generals, saying, "Excellent! Well done! Your wish to protect and bring happiness and peace to all sentient beings is an appropriate way to express your gratitude for the Medicine Buddha of Pure Crystal Radiance."

At that time, Ananda addressed the Buddha, "World-Honored One, from now on, how should we refer to this Dharma practice and how should we respectfully uphold it?" The Buddha responded to Ananda saying, "This Dharma practice is called the Virtuous Original Vows of Medicine Buddha of Pure Crystal Radiance, or can be also referred to as the Powerful Mantra and Wish-Weaving Twelve Yaksas Generals Benefiting Sentient Beings. This also may be referred to as The Practice of Removing All Karmic Obstructions. This is how it can be named and upheld."

After the Bhagavan had said these words, the entire assembly of all the bodhisattvas and great bodhisattvas and sravakas, kings and their subjects, brahmins, lay people, nagas, yaksas, gandharas, asuras, garudas, kinnaras, mahoragas, human and non-human beings, etc., were delighted to hear the words of the Buddha and faithfully received this teaching and practice.

"Namas Bhagavat Bhaisajyaguru Vaidurya Prabha Raja Tathagata Arhat Samyaksambuddha Tadyatha Om Bhaisajya Bhaishgajye Bhaishajya Samudgate Savha." (three times)

Praise to the Medicine Buddha

Medicine Buddha, the King of Extended Life,

please shine your radiant presence on this Dharma assembly
which resembles the moon's reflection in water.[86]

You who comes to the rescue of the suffering,

bestow your auspiciousness and remove all suffering
and dispel all disaster.

We are here to repent all wrongdoings committed in the three times.[87]

We pray for continuous good fortune and long life.

May the high, auspicious star shower the light of your kindness
upon us,

fulfilling our wishes and bringing peace and health.

May the high, auspicious star shower the light of your kindness
upon us,

fulfilling our wishes and bringing peace and health.

Medicine Buddha Gatha[88]

Medicine Buddha of Pure Crystal Radiance,
his magnificent flaming net without compare,
practices limitlessly his vow to benefit sentient beings
such that each has their wish fulfilled and never again regresses
on the spiritual path.
I take refuge in the Eastern Pure Land of the Medicine Buddha
of Pure Azure Radiance,
he who dispels disaster and extends life.
I take refuge in the Medicine Buddha,
he who dispels disaster and extends life.
I take refuge in the Radiant Sunlight Bodhisattva,
I take refuge in the Radiant Moonlight Bodhisattva.

Taking Refuge[89]

I take refuge in the Buddha, wishing all sentient beings
understand the Dharma and make the supreme vows.
I take refuge in the Dharma, wishing all sentient beings
study the sutras diligently and obtain prajna wisdom.
I take refuge in the Sangha, wishing all sentient beings
lead the public in harmony with no obstruction.

Transferring the Merits[90]

May kindness, compassion, joy, and equanimity
pervade all Dharma realms;
May all sentient beings benefit
from our blessings and friendship;
May our ethical practice of Chan and Pure Land
help us to realize equality and patience;
May we undertake the Great Vows
with humility and gratitude.

Notes

1 Sutra of Medicine Buddha: *Sanskrit (Skt.) "Bhagavan-bhaisajyaguru-vaiduryaprabhasya purvapranidhana-visesa-vistara;"* Chinese *(Ch.) "Yiao Shi Liuli Guang Rulai Benyuan Jing."* The most popular version was translated into Chinese by Xuanzang in 650 C.E. (T: vol. 14, no. 450). In addition to this version, there are two other translations in the Chinese Buddhist Canon. One was translated by Dharmagupta in 615 C.E. (T: vol.14, no. 449); the other was translated by Yijing in 707 C.E. (T: vol. 14, no. 451).

2 Thus, I have heard: *Skt. "evam maya srutam."* The opening sentence of sutras. The reason this is used as the starting comment of sutras is that before the Buddha attained parinirvana, he told his disciple, Ananda, to recite this phrase in order to discriminate between his teachings and others'. "Thus" indicates the teachings, sayings, or behaviors described in the content. "I have heard" indicates that Ananda truly attended the Dharma assembly and heard that the teachings were discoursed by Sakyamuni Buddha.

3 One time: *Skt. "ekasmim samaye."* It is usually followed by "Thus, I have heard," and it indicates the time when the Buddha was teaching the Dharma. The place, the event or subject, the participants are all described next to "One time."

4 Bhagavan: Or Bhagavat. One of ten epithets of Buddha. Literally, it means "fortunate, prosperous, happy, divine, adorable, and venerable. Because the Buddha has already eliminated all affliction and unwholesomeness, and attained enlightenment, he is the most venerable one.

5 Vaisali: One of sixteen kingdoms and also one of six big cities in ancient India. It is located on the northern shore of the Ganges River. Sakyamuni Buddha discoursed his teachings in Vaisali several times, including this sutra and the Vimalakirti Sutra. Additionally, the Second

Council in Buddhist history gathered here in 383 B.C.E.

6 Joyful Tree of Musical Breezes: According to descriptions contained within sutras, this kind of tree only exists in Pure Lands of Buddhas. It gives forth music to the breeze.

7 bhiksus: The male members of the Buddhist Sangha who have renounced the household life and received full ordination. The female members are called *"bhiksunis."* According to the Treatise on Perfection of Great Wisdom, literally, the word *"bhiksu"* can be traced back to the word *"bhiks"* (begging) and the word of *"bhinna-klesa"* (eliminating afflictions). Therefore, bhiksus/bhiksunis are also known as beggars or the ones who eliminate afflictions.

8 bodhisattva: The enlightening being. It is a compound word made up of "bodhi" and "sattva." Bodhi means enlightened, and sattva refers to sentient beings. Therefore, the word bodhisattva refers to one who is seeking the attainment of Buddhahood or liberation, and who practices all perfections. Bodhisattvas remain in the world to help others achieve enlightenment. The concept of bodhisattva is the main feature of Mahayana Buddhism.

9 great bodhisattvas: *Skt. "Mahasattvas."* Literally, *"maha"* means great; *"sattva"* indicates being, existence, reality, or entity. In Buddhism, "mahasattvas" refers to those sentient beings who have made great vows, are highly cultivated, and who help many other sentient beings reach liberation. Among worldly people, they are the supreme ones.

10 brahmins: In ancient India, the highest of four castes. Traditionally, they were the teachers and interpreters of religious knowledge. They were also the priests who acted as intermediaries between god, the world, and humans. In ancient Indian society, they were the only group allowed to change and perform the rituals of worship.

11 a constellation of celestial beings: Eight groups of celestial beings, including devas, nagas, yaksas, asuras, garudas, gandharvas, kinnaras, and mahoragas. 1) Devas: gods who reside above the human realm and between the heavens. They are still unenlightened and therefore subject to the cycle of birth and death (samsara). 2) Nagas: serpents or dragons that are beneficial half-divine beings that climb into the heavens in spring and live deep in the earth in winter. 3) Yaksas: swift powerful ghosts, which are usually harmful, but sometimes act as protectors of the Dharma. 4) Asuras: angry and contentious celestial beings who continually fight with the god Indra in Indian mythology. They are said to live at the bottom of the oceans surrounding Mt. Sumeru. 5) Garudas: celestial birds with strong large wings. 6) Gandharvas: celestial musicians associated with the court of the celestial monarch Indra. 7) Kinnaras: also known as kimnaras, they are also celestial musicians. They have a horse-like head with one horn and a human-like body. Males sing and females dance. 8) Mahoragas: beings shaped like boas or great snakes. These eight classes are all the parts of the retinue of Sakyamuni Buddha and of the Dharma protectors.

12 Dharma Prince Manjusri: Also known as Manjusri Bodhisattva or the Bodhisattva of Great Wisdom. He has the wisdom to see the true nature of all dharmas (phenomena). He is usually depicted as a youth, which reflects his capacity for refreshing clarity and insight.

13 baring his right shoulder and bowing upon his right knee with joined palms: The postures showing high respect in ancient India. When bhiksus go to see the Buddha or elders, they usually bare the right shoulder while the kasaya (robe) covers the left shoulder. This means "to serve," or "to obey the orders of laboring." "Bowing upon the right knee" is also a bodily manifestation of profound respect in Indian protocol when one goes to see the king. "Joined palms" (Skt. anjali) implies concentrating the mind and bowing with high respect. Traced back to Indian tradition, originally, Indians think that the right hand is sacred; the left hand is impure. If the right and left hand join into one, it means that the sides of the sacred and the impure in one's mind combine into one. By this gesture, Indians express the original face of human being. Buddhism adapted this gesture for not only expressing respect to others, but also asking one's self to return the original face, which is different from the original meaning and refers to one's true nature (Buddha Nature).

14 World-Honored One: One of ten epithets of Buddha. Traced back to the original Sanskrit term, *"loka-natha"* refers to the lord of the worlds, or *"loka-jyestha"* means the most venerable of the world. Today, it is usually translated as "the World-Honored One."

15 Sentient beings: *Skt. "sattvas."* The beings with consciousness, including the celestial beings, asuras, humans, animals, hungry ghosts, and hellish beings. From the Mahayana view, all sentient beings inherently have Buddha Nature, and therefore possess the capacity to attain enlightenment.

16 the Period of Semblance Dharma: The second period of Dharma influence. In total, there are three periods. 1) The Period of Right Dharma: *Skt. "saddharma."* This is the time when the Buddha still lived in this world and presented his teachings. During this period, a lot of people attained enlightenment after listening to the Buddha's teachings and practicing them. 2) The Period of Semblance Dharma: *Skt. "saddharma-pratirupaka."* This is the time when the Buddha's teachings are practiced, but enlightenment is seldom attained. 3) The Period of Declining Dharma: *Skt. "saddharma-vipralopa."* This is the time when the teachings still exist, but enlightenment is very rarely attained.

17 the Land of Pure Azure: The Pure Land of the Medicine Buddha, which is established by the power of the Medicine Buddha's twelve great vows. "Pure Azure" implies that this Pure Land has the qualities of clarity and radiance, such as that of the precious gem.

18 Medicine Buddha of Pure Azure Radiance: *Skt. "Bhaisajyaguru."*

Also known as the Buddha of Healing. In previous lives, when he practiced the bodhisattva path, he made twelve great vows to help sentient beings eliminate the suffering of physical and mental illness, and to guide them towards liberation. Usually, when the Medicine Buddha is depicted, his left hand holds the medicine bowl and his right hand is in the gesture of protection.

19 Worthy of Offerings: *Skt. "arhat" or "arhant"; Pali "arahat" or "arahant."* One of ten epithets of Buddha. The Buddha completed all virtues and reached ultimate wisdom and is free from all delusions and suffering. Therefore, the Buddha is worthy of offerings from heavenly and human beings.

20 Absolute Universal Enlightened Awareness: One of ten epithets of Buddha. *Skt. "samyaksambodhi;" Pali, "sammasambodhi."* "*Sambodhi*" refers to true wisdom, which enables one to see the true nature of all dharmas. This kind of wisdom is also known as the wisdom of Tathagata. *"Samyaksambodhi"* refers to the completely perfect knowledge and wisdom that all Buddhas are awakened to.

21 Activity of Bright Fullness: One of ten epithets of Buddha. *Skt. "vidya-carana-sampanna."* "Bright fullness" represents the unexcelled enlightenment (*anuttara-samyak-sambodhi*); and "activity" refers to the conduct based upon fulfilling precepts, meditation, and wisdom. Therefore, it can be said that the Buddha attained the supreme enlightenment, resulting from the perfect completion of upholding precepts, meditation, and wisdom.

22 Immaculately Departed One: One of ten epithets of Buddha. *Skt. "sugata."* Also known as "Well-Gone." It means to enter the state of deep samadhi and wonderful wisdom. In other words, the Buddha went to the other shore and has never been subject to the sea of birth and death again.

23 Transcendent Understanding of the Ordinary World: One of ten epithets of Buddha. *Skt. "lokavid."* The Buddha knows everything in the ordinary world, including that which is associated with sentient beings and non-sentient beings. He also understands the cause of formation of the mundane world as well as its extinction. On the other hand, he truly knows the path leading to the supramundane world.

24 Unexcelled One: One of ten epithets of Buddha. *Skt. "anuttara."* The virtues and wisdom of Tathagata are unexcelled in the mundane world.

25 The True Man Who Tames and Harmonizes: One of ten epithets of Buddha. *Skt. "purusa damyasarathi."* It means that the Buddha is the master who uses various kinds of skillful means, great loving-kindness, compassion, and wisdom to tame and guide sentient beings on the path leading to liberation.

26 Teacher of Divine and Human Beings: One of ten epithets of Buddha. *Skt. "sasta deva-manusyanam."* The Buddha teaches all sentient beings, including the celestial and human beings, what should be done and what should not, what is wholesome and what is not. The Buddha can also tell if one can follow his teachings, truly practice, not abandon Dharma and the path, and ultimately be free from afflictions.

27 Awakened One: Skt. "Buddha."

28 Anuttara-Samyak-Sambodhi: In Pali, *"anuttara-sammasambodhi."* The word *"anuttara"* means the supreme or the unexcelled (please see note of "unexcelled one"); "samyak-sambodhi" refers to the supreme perfect awakening or the full enlightenment.

29 the thirty-two marks of excellence: Also known as "the thirty-two excellent marks of the Buddha." *Skt. "dvatrimsanmaha purusa laksanani."* They are the remarkable physical characteristics possessed by a Buddha; they are the symbols of qualities attained at the highest level of cultivation. They are the following: 1) level feet, 2) symbols of a wheel on the soles of feet and on two hands, 3) long and slender fingers, 4) broad heels, 5) curved toes and fingers, 6) soft and smooth hands and feet, 7) arched feet, 8) lower body like an antelope's, 9) arms reaching to the knee, 10) virile member without narrowing in the fore-skin, 11) powerful body, 12) hairy body, 13) thick and curly body hair, 14) golden-hued body, 15) a body that gives off rays ten feet in every direction, 16) soft skin, 17) rounded hands, shoulders, and head, 18) well-formed shoulders, 19) upper body like a lion's, 20) erect body, 21) forty teeth, 22) powerful and muscular shoulders, 23) even teeth, 24) white teeth, 25) cheeks like a lion's, 26) the wonderful taste for all foods, 27) broad tongue, 28) voice like a Brahma's, 29) clear and blue eyes, 30) eyelashes like a bull's, 31) a cone-shaped elevation on the crown of the head, 32) a lock of hair between the eyebrows. (*Fo Guang Encyclopedia,* pages 507 ~ 511 & the *Shambhala Dictionary of Buddhism and Zen*)

30 the eighty noble qualities: Also known as "eighty accessory marks." *Skt. "asity-anuvyanjanani."* The minor characteristics of Buddhas or bodhisattvas.

31 a magnificent incendiary net of glory: This indicates the shining glory of the Buddha.

32 skillful means: *Skt. "upaya."* One of the ten perfections.

33 Bodhi: It means enlightenment. In the state of bodhi, one is awak-ened to the true nature of self; one is enlightened to one's own Buddha Nature. He/She has already eliminated all afflictions and delusions, and achieved prajna wisdom.

34 the sravaka or pratyeka-buddha vehicle: Literally, the word "sravaka" means hearer, and it refers to one who has attained enlightenment after listening to the Buddha's teachings; "pratyeka-bud-dha" refers to one who awakens to the Truth through their own efforts when they live in the time without a Buddha's presence. In the Mahayana view, these two belong to the small vehicle.

35 the great vehicle: Mahayana; the bodhisattva vehicle.

36 the Tri-Vidhani Silani: This term refers to Mahayana bodhisattva precepts, of which there are three kinds: 1) *Skt. "Samvara-sila"*: the bodhisattva precepts such as the five precepts, eight precepts, ten precepts, and the precepts of full ordination. The purpose is for sentient beings to engage in wholesomeness and prevent wrongdoing (F.G.E., p.6847-6848). 2) *Skt. "kusala-dharma-samgrahaka-sila"*: the precept vowing to fulfill all wholesome Dharma and to uphold all other precepts leading to Buddhahood (F.G.E., p.6849-6850). 3) *Skt. "sattvartha-kriya-sila"*: the precept of being beneficial to other sentient beings (F.G.E., p.6849).

37 the many disadvantages of the female form: In the original Chinese context, there are "one hundred disadvantages" mentioned. (Please see the *Yuye Sutra Discoursed by the Buddha* (T. Vol. 2, no. 142 & 143) or *Sattbhariya* in the Pali Canon for associated information.)

38 heterodox practices: Indicating the practices of seeking magical power or liberation from an external source.

39 all the bodhisattvas' disciplines: This refers to all practices of the bodhisattva path, including all the perfections (paramitas). Among the perfections, the most well known are the "six perfections," which are giving, upholding the precepts, patience, diligence, meditation, and prajna-wisdom.

40 the power of my awe-inspiring spiritual elan: Buddhas have perfectly completed unlimited merits, virtues, and qualities. Any one of these (merits, virtues, or qualities) has the great power to liberate sentient beings from suffering.

41 kalpas: The measuring unit of time in ancient India; a kalpa is an immense and inconceivable length of time. Buddhism adapts it to refer the period of time between the creation and recreation of the worlds.

42 no women's forms: No male-female dichotomy.

43 the Western Pure Land: Also known as the "Western Pure Land of Ultimate Bliss." It is created by the forty-eight great vows and great compassion of Amitabha Buddha. Through single-minded recitation of Amitabha Buddha's name, one can be reborn there through the transformation of a lotus flower. Once reborn in the Western Pure Land, one's practice is uninhibited and their path to enlightenment is without obstacle.

44 Radiant Sunlight Bodhisattva: *Skt. "Suryaprabha Bodhisattva."* One of the two attendants of Medicine Buddha. This Bodhisattva's physical manifestation is red and his right hand holds the sun wheel while the left hand holds a red flower.

45 Radiant Moonlight Bodhisattva: *Skt. "Candraprabha Bodhisattva."* The other attendant of Medicine Buddha. This Bodhisattva's physical manifestation is white. He sits on a swan and holds the moon wheel in his hand.

46 Yaksas or raksasas: For *"yaksa,"* please see the endnote "a constel-lation of celestial beings." The female yaksa is called *"yaksini."* *"Raksasa"* is the name of one type of bad ghost; the female is called *"raksasi."*

47 the eight purification precepts: Precepts are the rules of conduct and discipline established by the Buddha. Sakyamuni Buddha estab-lished the eight purification precepts for the purpose of offering the laity an opportunity to live in the monastery for one day-and-night to learn and experience the monastic life. They are the basic five pre-cepts with three additional disciplines: 1) no killing; 2) no stealing; 3) no sexual conduct; 4) no lying; 5) no intoxicants; 6) no using perfume and no singing or dancing; 7) no sleeping on a high or big bed; 8) no eating food during non-regulated hours.

48 Amitabha Buddha: The Buddha of Infinite Light. Also known as Amita Buddha or Amitayus Buddha (the Buddha of Infinite Life.)

49 Avalokitesvara Bodhisattva: One of the great bodhisattvas in Mahayana Buddhism. Avalokitesvara Bodhisattva can manifest in any conceivable form to bring help to whoever is in need. In Chinese Buddhism, Avalokitesvara is one of the four great bodhisattvas and is usually portrayed in the female form, known as "Kuan Yin" (Guanyin).

50 Maha Bodhisattva of Great Power to Heal and Save: Mahasthamaprapta Bodhisattva; also known as the Bodhisattva of Great Effort, who is the other attendant of Amitabha Buddha. This Bodhisattva brightens the universe with the light of wisdom and sits on the red lotus, holding a lotus flower in the left hand.

51 Unlimited Intention of Meaning Bodhisattva: Aksayamatir Bodhisattva. Literally, "*aksaya*" means unlimited, boundless, or infinite; "*matir*" is from "*mati,*" which means wisdom. Therefore, Aksayamatir is also known as the Bodhisattva of Infinite Wisdom.

52 the Medicine King Bodhisattva: Bhaisajyaraja Bodhisattva. Considered a Bodhisattva of Healing, he gives sentient beings medicine to heal mental and physical illness.

53 the Supreme Medicine Bodhisattva: *Bhaisajya-samudgata Bodhisattva.* Along with the Medicine King Bodhisattva, he is also a Bodhisattva of Healing.

54 Maitreya Bodhisattva: The next Buddha, said to be the one who will succeed Sakyamuni Buddha in this world. At present, Maitreya Bodhisattva is in Tusita Heaven expounding the Dharma to the heavenly beings in the inner palace.

55 a cakravartin: Also known as "*cakravartirajan*;" a virtuous, noble, and powerful king in Indian mythology who is said to be able to compassionately and skillfully rule the whole world.

56 the four continents: According to Buddhist cosmology, the continent of Jambudvipa is in the South; the continent of Purvavideha is in the East; the continent of Aparagodana is in the West; and the continent of Uttarakuru is in the North. At the center of the four continents is Mt. Sumeru.

57 the ten good ways: Also known as the ten wholesome conducts, which are no killing, no stealing, no sexual misconduct, no lying, no duplicity, no harsh words, no flattery, no greed, no hatred or anger, and no ignorance.

58 a kasatriya: The second of four castes in ancient Indian society. It is the warrior and ruling class.

59 samadhi: Literally, "establish, or make firm." It means concentration; a state in which the mind is concentrated in a one-pointed focus and all mental activities are calm. In samadhi, one is free from all distractions, thereby entering a state of inner serenity.

60 dharani: Also known as "mantra" or "spell." Literally, it means "uniting and holding," which further extends to "uniting all dharmas and holding all meanings."

61 Namas: Pali. "namo." It means "to submit oneself to" or " to take refuge in."

62 Bhaisajyaguru Vaidurya Prabha Raja Tathagata: The complete Sanskrit title of the Medicine Buddha.

63 Arhat: When referring to the Buddha, it means Worthy of Offerings; it is one of the ten epithets of a Buddha. (please see note on "Worthy of Offerings") In general, an arhat is one who has been devoted to attaining enlightenment and liberation from the cycle of birth for oneself. This self-liberation is in contrast to the path of the bodhisattva who seeks liberation for all beings.

64 Samyaksambuddha: "The One of Absolute Universal Enlightened Awareness."

65 Om: Literally, "holy"; it is usually put in the beginning of the prayer.

66 Bhasisajya: "Medicine."

67 Svaha: The word at the end of a dharani (mantra). It contains the meaning of the intention of the dharani, whether an achievement or accomplishment, or the intention of ending disasters and gaining benefits.

68 the teeth-cleaning twig: In ancient India, people used a twig to clean their teeth and to keep their mouth fresh.

69 the Four Heavenly Kings: According to Buddhist cosmology, there are four mythical kings who live halfway down Mt. Sumeru. King Dhatarastra is in the East; King Virudhaka is in the South; King Virupaksa is in the West; and King Dhanada (or Vaisravana) is in the North.

70 loving-kindness, compassion, joy, equanimity: Four immeasurable states of mind.

71 the five precepts: The most basic moral precepts in Buddhism; they are no killing, no stealing, no lying, no sexual misconduct, and no intoxicants.

72 the ten precepts: The ten precepts are a further expansion of the eight purification precepts. The first five precepts are the same, and the rest are: 6) no wearing adornments or perfume; 7) no singing or dancing; 8) no sleeping on a high or large bed; 9) no eating after noon; 10) no possessing gold, silver, or other precious metals and jewels.

73 the three lower realms upon rebirth: The three realms of animal, hungry ghost, and hell.

74 Ananda: One of ten great disciples of the Buddha. He is noted as the foremost in hearing and learning. After the Buddha entered parinirvana, Ananda is said to have compiled the sutras in Vaibhara Cave, which is in Magadha, India, and which is where the five hundred disciples of the Buddha were assembled.

75 the ten stages of bodhisattva development: "The ten stages" are also known as "the ten grounds," which are from the forty-first to the fiftieth level in the fifty-two levels of the bodhisattva path. These are the stages through which a Buddhist practitioner progresses.

76 Only those bodhisattvas who will attain Buddhahood in their next lifetime: *Skt. "Ekajatipratibaddha."* Refers to fifty-first level bodhisattvas who are called the Bodhisattvas of Equal Enlightenment.

77 the Triple Gem: The Buddha, the Dharma, and the Sangha.

78 Rescuing Aid Bodhisattva: This Bodhisattva frees sentient beings from the suffering of illness and disaster. His physical manifestation is red and he sits on a lotus seat.

79 the Judgment King of Hell: Skt. *"Yama"* or *"Yama-raja."*

80 seven layers of lamps: In Buddhism, lighting a lamp and offering it to the Buddha or the Sangha can help one gain a lot of merits.

81 the five-colored longevity banners: *Skt. "pataka."* In Buddhism, making and displaying a banner can help one accumulate various blessings and virtues. It also can express the Buddhas' or bodhisattvas' great power to tame maras, which, in Buddhism, are considered to be human passions or temptations that hinder one's practice.

82 seven, twenty-one, thirty-five, or forty-nine days: According to Buddhism, in the state between death and rebirth (also called "inter-state"), consciousness is still active and exists. Here it has a lifespan of seven days, which can repeat up to seven times (forty-nine days). After the first seven days, consciousness experiences death —it is waiting for the right conditions for rebirth. If the conditions are not right, consciousness will be reborn into the second stage. After the longest stage of forty-nine days, consciousness must move on from the inter-state and be reborn.

83 Great Virtuous One: *Skt. "Bhadanta."* In India, it is a respectful title used to address the Buddha, bodhisattvas, or Dharma teachers.

84 forty-nine three-finger-length sections: The unit to measure length in ancient India. One section is about 23 cm.

85 the five violations: They are parricide, matricide, killing an arhat, shedding the blood of a Buddha, and destroying the harmony of the Sangha.

86 Dharma assembly which resembles the moon's reflection in water: Used to describe that a Dharma assembly is held due to the need for cultivating sentient beings. It does not exist forever, and because it relies on conditions — as everything does — it will change. It will not be permanent, similar to the moon's reflection in water.

87 the three times: The past, present, and future.

88 Gatha: verse

89 Take Refuge: *Skt. "sarana."* The Sanskrit term literally means liberating, helping, and protecting. To "Take Refuge" means that by relying on the virtuous power of the Triple Gem, one who takes refuge can eliminate suffering and be free from the cycle of birth and death.

90 Transferring Merits: *Skt. "Parinama."* In Buddhism, it is the last step in any kind of ceremony or recitation of sutras, a Buddha's name, or a dharani.

A Prayer to
the Medicine Buddha

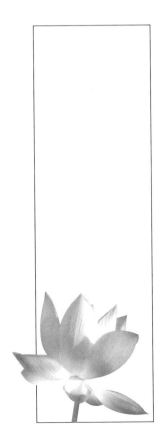

A Prayer to the Medicine Buddha

Oh great, compassionate Medicine Buddha,
Please listen to my report:
There is truly too much suffering
In the world nowadays;
The violations of burning,
Killing, and plundering,
The cruel oppression of corrupt officials,
The turbulence of politics and the economy,
The disasters of earth, water, fire, and wind;
All these often make people lose
Everything they own
In the blink of an eye.
The anguish of being bedridden
With a lingering illness
Resulting from an imbalance
Of the four elements;
Even heroes moan and groan
And have difficulty being at ease;
The sea of karma
That is full
Of passions and delusions
Resulting from greed,
Anger, and ignorance
Rolls unceasingly like
Roaring waves and billows.

Oh great, compassionate Medicine Buddha,
If we do not depend on you now,
How can we come out
Of the sea of misery?

If we do not rely on you now,
How can we subdue
The evil of resentment?
Today, I sincerely chant your name,
Pay respect to your holy face,
Not to pray to you
Only to bless myself,
But to hope that all beings
Obtain your protection
To live and work
In peace and contentment
And in happiness and harmony.

Oh great, compassionate Medicine Buddha,
We understand thoroughly:
That, in this evil world
Of the five Kasaya periods of impurity,
All natural disasters
And man-made calamities
Are caused by collective karma;
That, on this filthy, mundane earth,
Physical and mental suffering
Is caused
By the passions and delusions of life.
If we want to thoroughly eliminate
Calamities and disasters,
We must first eliminate
Our own karma of wrongdoings;
If we want to establish
The Pure Land of the East,
We must first purify

Our bodies and minds.
Therefore,
I would like for you,
Medicine Buddha,
To eliminate
our greed and anger,
To eliminate
our ignorance and struggles.
We are willing to transfer
All our good-rooted merits
To all beings in the dharma realm.
May everyone be able to live freely
And everything turn out as they wish.

Furthermore,
Great, compassionate Medicine Buddha,
I pray to you to bestow
Your great power on us
For protection;
I will initiate the following,
Pure, original vows:
First vow: May all sentient beings
Be equal and at ease;
Second vow: May all undertakings
Benefit the masses;
Third vow: May panic and horror
Be kept far away;
Fourth vow: May all sentient beings
Calmly uphold bodhi;
Fifth vow: May man-made calamities
And natural disasters

Disappear completely;
Sixth vow: May all disabled beings
Be rehabilitated back to normal;
Seventh vow: May all beings
Suffering from diseases
Be restored to health;
Eighth vow: May all human relations
Foster mutual understanding and harmony;
Ninth vow: May all beings with evil views
Turn over a new leaf;
Tenth vow: May all prisoners
Suffering unjustly
Reverse the situation of injustice;
Eleventh vow: May society and the masses
Live in affluence;
Twelfth vow: May all beings
Be tolerant and respectful.

Oh great, compassionate Medicine Buddha,
We make offerings to you
With our pure karma
Of body, speech, and mind;
We take you as our model
With our diligent progress
In the study of discipline,
Meditation, and wisdom;
I pray that you give,
With your great compassion,
Your respect-inspiring virtues
All over the dharma realm
To fulfill our wishes,

To let our human world also
Be able to establish
The Pure Land of the East.

Oh great, compassionate Medicine Buddha,
Please accept my sincerest prayer!
Please accept my sincerest prayer!

Chinese and English Phonetic Pronunciation

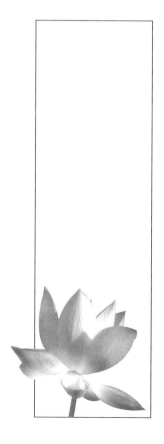

LU XIANG ZAN
爐 香 讚

LU	XIANG	ZHA	RE			
爐	香	乍	熱			

FA	JIE	MENG	XUN			
法	界	蒙	薰			

ZHU	FO	HAI	HUI	XI	YAO	WEN
諸	佛	海	會	悉	遙	聞

SUI	CHU	JIE	XIANG	YUN		
隨	處	結	祥	雲		

CHENG	YI	FANG	YIN			
誠	意	方	殷			

ZHU	FO	XIAN	QUAN	SHENG		
諸	佛	現	全	身		

NAN	MO	XIANG	YUN	GAI	PU	SA	MO
南	無	香	雲	蓋	菩	薩	摩

HE	SA					
訶	薩	(三 遍) (3 TIMES)				

63

NAN	MO	XIAO	ZAI	YAN	SHOU	YAO	SHI
南	無	消	災	延	壽	藥	師

FO
佛

(三 遍) (3 TIMES)

KAI　JING　JI
開　經　偈

WU	SHANG	SHEN	SHEN	WEI	MIAO	FA
無	上	甚	深	微	妙	法
BAI	QIAN	WAN	JIE	NAN	ZAO	YU
百	千	萬	劫	難	遭	遇
WO	JIN	JIAN	WEN	DE	SHOU	CHI
我	今	見	聞	得	受	持
YUAN	JIE	RU	LAI	ZHEN	SHI	YI
願	解	如	來	真	實	義

YAO SHI LIU LI GUANG RU LAI BEN YUAN GONG DE JING
藥師琉璃光如來本願功德經

```
            RU    SHI    WO    WEN          YI
            如     是     我     聞    ：     一

SHI   BAO   QIE   FAN   YOU   HUA   ZHU   GUO
時     薄     伽     梵     遊     化     諸     國

      ZHI  GUANG  YAN  CHENG        ZHU   YUE
。     至     廣     嚴     城     ，     住     樂

YIN   SHU   XIA          YU    DA    BI    CHU
音     樹     下     。     與     大     苾     芻

ZHONG BA    QIAN  REN   JU          PU    SA
眾     八     千     人     俱     ，     菩     薩

MO    HE    SA    SAN   WAN   LIU   QIAN
摩     訶     薩     三     萬     六     千     ，

JI    GUO  WANG         DA    CHEN        PO
及     國     王     、     大     臣     、     婆

LUO   MEN          JU    SHI         TIAN  LONG
羅     門     、     居     士     、     天     龍

BA    BU           REN   FEI   REN   DENG
八     部     、     人     非     人     等     ，

WU   LIANG   DA   ZHONG        GONG  JING  WEI
無     量     大     眾     ，     恭     敬     圍
```

65

繞，而為說法。

爾時，曼殊室利法王子，承佛威神，從座而起，偏袒一肩，右膝著地，向薄伽梵曲躬合掌，白言：「世尊！惟願演說如是相類諸佛名號，及本大願殊勝功德，令諸聞者，業障消除，為欲利樂像法轉時，諸有情故。」

爾時，世尊讚

曼殊室利童子言：

「善哉！善哉！曼殊

室利！汝以大悲，

勸請我說諸佛名號

，本願功德，為拔

業障所纏有情，利

益安樂像法轉時，

諸有情故。汝今諦

聽，極善思惟，當

為汝說。」

67

MAN SHU SHI LI YAN：
曼　殊　室　利　言　：

WEI RAN 　 YUAN SHUO 　 WO DENG
「唯　然　！　願　說　，　我　等

YAO WEN
樂　聞　。」

　 FO GAO MAN SHU SHI LI
　 佛　告　曼　殊　室　利

　 DONG FANG QU CI GUO SHI QING
：「 東　方　去　此　過　十　殑

QIE SHA DENG FO TU 　 YOU SHI
伽　沙　等　佛　土　，　有　世

JIE MING JING LIU LI 　 FO HAO
界　名　淨　琉　璃　，　佛　號

YAO SHI LIU LI GUANG YU LAI
藥　師　琉　璃　光　如　來　、

YING 　 ZHENG DENG JUE 　 MING XING
應　、　正　等　覺　、　明　行

YUAN MAN 　 SHAN SHI 　 SHI JIAN
圓　滿　、　善　逝　、　世　間

JIE 　 WU SHANG SHI 　 DIAO YU
解　、　無　上　士　、　調　御

ZHANG FU 　 TIAN REN SHI 　 FO
丈　夫　、　天　人　師　、　佛

68

、薄伽梵。曼殊室利！彼世尊藥師琉璃光如來本行菩薩道時，發十二大願，令諸有情所求皆得。

第一大願，願我來世得阿耨多羅三藐三菩提時，自身光明，熾然照耀無量無數無邊世界。以三十二大丈夫相、八十隨形，莊嚴其身；令一切有情，如我無異。

第二大願，願我來世得菩提時，身如琉璃，內外明徹，淨無瑕穢，光明廣大，功德巍巍，身善安住，焰網莊嚴，過於日月；幽冥眾生，悉蒙開曉，隨意所趣，作

諸事業 。

第三大願 ，願

我來世得菩提時 ，

以無量無邊智慧方

便 ，令諸有情皆得

無盡所受用物 ，莫

令眾生有所乏少 。

第四大願 ，願

我來世得菩提時 ，

若諸有情行邪道者

，悉令安住菩提道

中；若行聲聞獨覺

乘者，皆以大乘而安立之。

第五大願，願我來世得菩提時，若有無量無邊有情，於我法中修行梵行，一切皆令得不缺戒，具三聚戒；設有毀犯，聞我名已，還得清淨，不墮惡趣。

第六大願，願

我來世得菩提時，若諸有情其身下劣，諸根不具，醜陋、頑愚、盲聾瘖瘂、攣躄背僂、白癩癲狂、種種病苦；聞我名已，一切皆得端正黠慧，諸根完具，無諸疾苦。

第七大願，願我來世得菩提時，若諸有情，眾病逼

73

切，無救無歸，無醫無藥，無親無家，貧窮多苦；我之名號，一經其耳，眾病悉除，身心安樂，家屬資具，悉皆豐足，乃至證得無上菩提。

第八大願，願我來世得菩提時，若有女人，為女百惡之所逼惱，極生厭離，願捨女身；聞我名已，一切皆得轉女成男，具丈夫相，乃至證得無上菩提。

第九大願，願我來世得菩提時，令諸有情，出魔羂網，解脫一切外道纏縛；若墮種種惡見稠林，皆當引攝置於正見，漸令修習諸菩薩行，速證無上正等菩提。

第十大願，願我來世得菩提時，若諸有情，王法所錄，繩縛鞭撻，繫閉牢獄；或當刑戮，及餘無量災難陵辱，悲愁煎逼，身心受苦；若聞我名，以我福德威神力故，皆得解脫一切

YOU KU
憂 苦 。

DI SHI YI DA YUAN
第 十 一 大 願 ，

YUAN WO LAI SHI DE PU TI SHI
願 我 來 世 得 菩 提 時 ，

RUO ZHU YOU QING JI KE
若 諸 有 情 ， 飢 渴

SUO NAO WEI QIU SHI GU
所 惱 ， 為 求 食 故 ，

ZAO ZHU E YE DE WEN WO
造 諸 惡 業 ； 得 聞 我

MING ZHUAN NIAN SHOU CHI WO
名 ， 專 念 受 持 ， 我

DANG XIAN YI SHANG MIAO YIN SHI
當 先 以 上 妙 飲 食 ，

BAO ZU QI SHEN HOU YI FA
飽 足 其 身 ； 後 以 法

WEI BI JING AN LE ER JIAN
味 ， 畢 竟 安 樂 而 建

LI ZHI
立 之 。

DI SHI ER DA YUAN
第 十 二 大 願 ，

77

YUAN WO LAI SHI DE PU TI SHI
願我來世得菩提時，

RUO ZHU YOU QING PIN WU
若諸有情，貧無

YI FU WEN MENG HAN RE
衣服，蚊虻寒熱，

ZHOU YE BI NAO RUO WEN WO
晝夜逼惱；若聞我

MING ZHUAN NIAN SHOU CHI RU
名，專念受持，如

QI SUO HAO JI DE ZHONG ZHONG
其所好，即得種種

SHANG MIAO YI FU YI DE YI
上妙衣服，亦得一

QIE BAO ZHUANG YAN JU HUA MAN
切寶莊嚴具，華鬘

TU XIANG GU YUE ZHONG JI
塗香，鼓樂眾伎，

SUI XIN SUO WAN JIE LING MAN
隨心所翫，皆令滿

ZU
足。

MAN SHU SHI LI SHI
曼殊室利！是

WEI BI SHI ZUN YAO SHI LIU LI
為 彼 世 尊 藥 師 琉 璃

GUANG RU LAI 、 YING 、 ZHENG DENG
光 如 來 、 應 、 正 等

JUE ， XING PU SA DAO SHI ，
覺 ， 行 菩 薩 道 時 ，

SUO FA SHI ER WEI MIAO SHANG YUAN
所 發 十 二 微 妙 上 願

。

FU CI ， MAN SHU SHI
復 次 ， 曼 殊 室

LI ！ BI SHI ZUN YAO SHI LIU
利 ！ 彼 世 尊 藥 師 琉

LI GUANG RU LAI ， XING PU SA
璃 光 如 來 ， 行 菩 薩

DAO SHI ， SUO FA DA YUAN ，
道 時 ， 所 發 大 願 ，

JI BI FO TU GONG DE ZHUANG YAN
及 彼 佛 土 功 德 莊 嚴

， WO RUO YI JIE ， RUO YI
， 我 若 一 劫 ， 若 一

JIE YU ， SHUO BU NENG JIN 。
劫 餘 ， 說 不 能 盡 。

RAN 然　BI 彼　FO 佛　TU 土　，　YI 一

XIANG 向　QING 清　JING 淨　，　WU 無　YOU 有　NU 女　REN 人

，　YI 亦　WU 無　E 惡　QU 趣　JI 及　KU 苦　YIN 音

SHENG 聲　；　LIU 琉　LI 璃　WEI 為　DI 地　，　JIN 金

SHENG 繩　JIE 界　DAO 道　，　CHENG 城　QUE 闕　GONG 宮　GE 閣

，　XUAN 軒　CHUANG 窗　LUO 羅　WANG 網　，　JIE 皆　QI 七

BAO 寶　CHENG 成　。　YI 亦　RU 如　XI 西　FANG 方　JI 極

LE 樂　SHI 世　JIE 界　，　GONG 功　DE 德　ZHUANG 莊　YAN 嚴

，　DENG 等　WU 無　CHA 差　BIE 別　。　YU 於　QI 其

GUO 國　ZHONG 中　，　YOU 有　ER 二　PU 菩　SA 薩　MO 摩

HE 訶　SA 薩　，　YI 一　MING 名　RI 日　GUANG 光　BIAN 遍

ZHAO 照　，　ER 二　MING 名　YUE 月　GUANG 光　BIAN 遍　ZHAO 照

，是彼無量無數菩薩眾之上首，次補佛處，悉能持彼世尊藥師琉璃光如來正法寶藏。是故，曼殊室利！諸有信心善男子善女人等，應當願生彼佛世界。

爾時，世尊復告曼殊室利童子言：「曼殊室利！有諸

ZHONG SHENG ， BU SHI SHAN E ，
眾　生　，　不　識　善　惡　，

WEI HUAI TAN LIN ， BU ZHI BU
唯　懷　貪　吝　，　不　知　布

SHI ， JI SHI GUO BAO ； YU
施　，　及　施　果　報　；　愚

CHI WU ZHI ， QUE YU XIN GEN
癡　無　智　，　闕　於　信　根

， DUO JU CAI BAO ， QIN JIA
，　多　聚　財　寶　，　勤　加

SHOU HU ； JIAN QI ZHE LAI ，
守　護　；　見　乞　者　來　，

QI XIN BU XI ， SHE BU HUO
其　心　不　喜　，　設　不　獲

YI ER XING SHI SHI ， RU GE
已　而　行　施　時　，　如　割

SHEN ROU ， SHEN SHENG TONG XI 。
身　肉　，　深　生　痛　惜　。

FU YOU WU LIANG QIAN TAN YOU QING
復　有　無　量　慳　貪　有　情

， JI JI ZI CAI ， YU QI
，　積　集　資　財　，　於　其

ZI SHEN ， SHANG BU SHOU YONG ，
自　身　，　尚　不　受　用　，

HE 何	KUANG 況	NENG 能	YU 與	FU 父	MU 母	QI 妻	ZI 子
、	NU 奴	BI 婢	ZUO 作	SHI 使	、	JI 及	LAI 來
QI 乞	ZHE 者	！	BI 彼	ZHU 諸	YOU 有	QING 情	，
CONG 從	CI 此	MING 命	ZHONG 終	，	SHENG 生	E 餓	GUI 鬼
JIE 界	，	HUO 或	PANG 傍	SHENG 生	QU 趣	。	YOU 由
XI 昔	REN 人	JIAN 間	，	CENG 曾	DE 得	ZAN 暫	WEN 聞
YAO 藥	SHI 師	LIU 琉	LI 璃	GUANG 光	RU 如	LAI 來	MING 名
GU 故	，	JIN 今	ZAI 在	E 惡	QU 趣	，	ZAN 暫
DE 得	YI 憶	NIAN 念	BI 彼	RU 如	LAI 來	MING 名	，
JI 即	YU 於	NIAN 念	SHI 時	，	CONG 從	BI 彼	CHU 處
MO 沒	，	HUAN 還	SHENG 生	REN 人	ZHONG 中	。	DE 得
SU 宿	MING 命	NIAN 念	，	WEI 畏	E 惡	U 趣	KU 苦

83

，不(BU) 樂(YAO) 欲(YU) 樂(LE) ，好(HAO) 行(XING)
惠(HUI) 施(SHI) ，讚(ZAN) 歎(TAN) 施(SHI) 者(ZHE) ，
一(YI) 切(QIE) 所(SUO) 有(YOU) 悉(XI) 無(WU) 貪(TAN) 惜(XI)
，漸(JIAN) 次(CI) 尚(SHANG) 能(NENG) 以(YI) 頭(TOU) 目(MU)
、手(SHOU) 足(ZU) 、血(XUE) 肉(ROU) 、身(SHEN)
分(FEN) ，施(SHI) 來(LAI) 求(QIU) 者(ZHE) ，況(KUANG)
餘(YU) 財(CAI) 物(WU) 。

復(FU) 次(CI) ，曼(MAN) 殊(SHU) 室(SHI)
利(LI) ！若(RUO) 諸(ZHU) 有(YOU) 情(QING) ，雖(SUI)
於(YU) 如(RU) 來(LAI) 受(SHOU) 諸(ZHU) 學(XUE) 處(CHU) ，
而(ER) 破(PO) 尸(SHI) 羅(LUO) ；有(YOU) 雖(SUI) 不(BU)
破(PO) 尸(SHI) 羅(LUO) ，而(ER) 破(PO) 軌(GUI) 則(ZE)

；有於尸羅、軌則

，雖得不壞，然毀

正見 ；有雖不毀正

見，而棄多聞，於

佛所說契經深義不

能解了；有雖多聞

，而增上慢，由增

上慢覆蔽心故，自

是非他，嫌謗正法

，為魔伴黨。如是

愚人，自行邪見，

復令無量俱胝有情

，墮大險坑。此
有情、應於地獄、
傍生、鬼趣，流轉
無窮。若得聞此藥
師琉璃光如來名號
，便捨惡行，修諸
善法，不墮惡趣。
設有不能捨諸
惡行，修行善法，
墮惡趣者，以彼如
來本願威力，令其
現前暫聞名號，從

BI　MING　ZHONG　　　HUAN　SHENG　REN　QU
彼　命　終　，　還　生　人　趣

　　DE　ZHENG　JIAN　JING　JIN　　　SHAN
。　得　正　見　精　進　，　善

TIAO　YI　LE　　　BIAN　NENG　SHE　JIA
調　意　樂　，　便　能　捨　家

　　QU　YU　FEI　JIA　　　RU　LAI
，　趣　於　非　家　，　如　來

FA　ZHONG　　　SHOU　CHI　XUE　CHU
法　中　，　受　持　學　處　，

WU　YOU　HUI　FAN　　　ZHENG　JIAN　DUO
無　有　毀　犯　；　正　見　多

WEN　　　JIE　SHEN　SHEN　YI　　　LI
聞　，　解　甚　深　義　，　離

ZENG　SHANG　MAN　　　BU　BANG　ZHENG　FA
增　上　慢　，　不　謗　正　法

　　BU　WEI　MO　BAN　　　JIAN　CI
，　不　為　魔　伴　，　漸　次

XIU　XING　ZHU　PU　SA　XING　　　SU
修　行　諸　菩　薩　行　，　速

DE　YUAN　MAN
得　圓　滿　。

　　　　FU　CI　　　MAN　SHU　SHI
　　復　次　，　曼　殊　室

87

利！若諸有情，慳貪嫉妒，自讚毀他，當墮三惡趣中，無量千歲受諸劇苦；受劇苦已，從彼命終，來生人間，作牛馬駝驢，恆被鞭撻，飢渴逼惱；又常負重，隨路而行。或得為人，生居下賤，作人奴婢，受他驅役，恆不自在。若昔人中，曾聞世尊藥師琉璃光如來名號，由此善因，今復憶念，至心歸依。以佛神力，眾苦解脱，諸根聰利，智慧多聞，恆求勝法，常遇善友，永斷魔羂，破無明殼，竭煩惱河，解脱一切生老病死、憂愁苦惱。

復次，曼殊室利！若諸有情，好喜乖離，更相鬥訟，惱亂自他，以身語意，造作增長種種惡業，展轉常為不饒益事，互相謀害。告召山林樹塚等神，殺諸眾生，取其血肉，祭祀藥叉、羅剎婆等；書怨人名，作其形像

，	YI 以	E 惡	ZHOU 咒	SHU 術	ER 而	ZHOU 咒	ZU 詛
ZHI 之		YAN 厭	MEI 魅	GU 蠱	DAO 道	，	ZHOU 咒
QI 起	SHI 屍	GUI 鬼	，	LING 令	DUAN 斷	BI 彼	MING 命
，	JI 及	HUAI 壞	QI 其	SHEN 身	。	SHI 是	ZHU 諸
YOU 有	QING 情	，	RUO 若	DE 得	WEN 聞	CI 此	YAO 藥
SHI 師	LIU 琉	LI 璃	GUANG 光	RU 如	LAI 來	MING 名	HAO 號
，	BI 彼	ZHU 諸	E 惡	SHI 事	，	XI 悉	BU 不
NENG 能	HAI 害	。	YI 一	QIE 切	ZHAN 展	ZHUAN 轉	JIE 皆
QI 起	CI 慈	XIN 心	，	LI 利	YI 益	AN 安	LE 樂
，	WU 無	SUN 損	NAO 惱	YI 意	，	JI 及	XIAN 嫌
HEN 恨	XIN 心	；	GE 各	GE 各	HUAN 歡	YUE 悅	，
YU 於	ZI 自	SUO 所	SHOU 受	，	SHENG 生	YU 於	XI 喜

足，不相侵陵，互為饒益。復次，曼殊室利！若有四眾：苾芻、苾芻尼、鄔波索迦、鄔波斯迦，及餘淨信善男子、善女人等，有能受持八分齋戒。或經一年，或復三月，受持學處，以此善根願生西方極樂世

JIE 界　WU 無　LIANG 量　SHOU 壽　FO 佛　SUO 所　，　TING 聽

WEN 聞　ZHENG 正　FA 法　，　ER 而　WEI 未　DING 定　ZHE 者

。　RUO 若　WEN 聞　SHI 世　ZUN 尊　YAO 藥　SHI 師　LIU 琉

LI 璃　GUANG 光　RU 如　LAI 來　MING 名　HAO 號　，　LIN 臨

MING 命　ZHONG 終　SHI 時　，　YOU 有　BA 八　DA 大　PU 菩

SA 薩　，　QI 其　MING 名　YUE 曰　WEN 文　SHU 殊　SHI 師

LI 利　PU 菩　SA 薩　、　GUAN 觀　SHI 世　YIN 音　PU 菩

SA 薩　、　DE 得　DA 大　SHI 勢　PU 菩　SA 薩　、

WU 無　JIN 盡　YI 意　PU 菩　SA 薩　、　BAO 寶　TAN 檀

HUA 華　PU 菩　SA 薩　、　YAO 藥　WANG 王　PU 菩　SA 薩

、　YAO 藥　SHANG 上　PU 菩　SA 薩　、　MI 彌　LE 勒

PU 菩　SA 薩　。　SHI 是　BA 八　DA 大　PU 菩　SA 薩

CHENG KONG ER LAI SHI QI DAO
乘 空 而 來 ， 示 其 道

LU JI YU BI JIE ZHONG ZHONG
路 ， 即 於 彼 界 種 種

ZA SE ZHONG BAO HUA ZHONG CI
雜 色 眾 寶 華 中 ， 自

RAN HUA SHENG HUO YOU YIN CI
然 化 生 。 或 有 因 此

SHENG YU TIAN SHANG SUI SHENG TIAN
生 於 天 上 ， 雖 生 天

SHANG ER BEN SHAN GEN YI WEI
上 ， 而 本 善 根 亦 未

QIONG JIN BU FU GENG SHENG ZHU
窮 盡 ， 不 復 更 生 諸

YU E QU
餘 惡 趣 。

TIAN SHANG SHOU JIN HUAN
天 上 壽 盡 ， 還

SHENG REN JIAN HUO WEI LUN WANG
生 人 間 ， 或 為 輪 王

TONG SHE SI ZHOU WEI DE
， 統 攝 四 洲 ， 威 德

ZI CAI AN LI WU LIANG BAI
自 在 ， 安 立 無 量 百

千有情於十善道。或生剎帝利、婆羅門、居士、大家，多饒財寶，倉庫盈溢，形相端嚴，眷屬具足，聰明智慧，勇健威猛，如大力士。若是女人，得聞世尊藥師琉璃光如來名號，至心受持，於後不復更受女身。

復次，曼殊室

利！彼藥師琉璃光

如來得菩提時，由

本願力，觀諸有情

，遇眾病苦，瘦攣

、乾消、黃熱等病

；或被厭魅、蠱毒

所中；或復短命，

或時橫死；欲令是

等病苦消除，所求

願滿。

時彼世尊入三摩地，名曰除滅一切眾生苦惱。既入定已，於肉髻中，出大光明，光中演說大陀羅尼曰：「南無薄伽伐帝，鞞殺社，寠嚕薜琉璃缽喇婆，喝囉闍也，怛陀揭多耶，阿囉喝帝，三藐三勃陀耶，怛姪陀。唵！

韡殺逝，韡殺逝，

韡殺社！　三沒揭帝，

莎訶！

爾時，光中說

此咒已，大地震動，

放大光明，一切

眾生病苦皆除，受

安隱樂。

曼殊室利！若

見男子女人，有病

苦者，應當一心為

彼病人，常清淨澡

98

SHU　　　HUO　SHI　HUO　YAO　　　HUO
漱　，　或　食　或　藥　，　或

WU　CHONG　SHUI　　ZHOU　YI　BAI　BA
無　蟲　水　，　咒　一　百　八

BIAN　　YU　BI　FU　SHI　　SUO
遍　，　與　彼　服　食　，　所

YOU　BING　KU　　XI　JIE　XIAO　MIE
有　病　苦　，　悉　皆　消　滅

。　RUO　YOU　SUO　QIU　　ZHI　XIN
　　若　有　所　求　，　至　心

NIAN　SONG　　JIE　DE　RU　SHI　WU
念　誦　，　皆　得　如　是　無

BING　YAN　NIAN　　MING　ZHONG　ZHI　HOU
病　延　年　；　命　終　之　後

，　SHENG　BI　SHI　JIE　　DE　BU
，　生　彼　世　界　，　得　不

TUI　ZHUAN　　NAI　ZHI　PU　TI
退　轉　，　乃　至　菩　提　。

SHI　GU　　MAN　SHU　SHI　LI
是　故　，　曼　殊　室　利　！

RUO　YOU　NAN　ZI　NU　REN　　YU
若　有　男　子　女　人　，　於

BI　YAO　SHI　LIU　LI　GUANG　RU　LAI
彼　藥　師　琉　璃　光　如　來

99

，至心殷重，恭敬
供養者，常持此咒
，勿令廢忘。

復次，曼殊室
利！若有淨信男子
女人，得聞藥師琉
璃光如來、應、正
等覺所有名號，聞
已誦持，晨嚼齒木
，澡漱清淨，以諸
香華、燒香、塗香
，作眾伎樂，供養

形像。於此經典，若自書，若教人書，一心受持，聽聞其義，於彼法師，應修供養，一切所有資身之具，悉皆施與，勿令乏少。如是，便蒙諸佛護念，所求願滿，乃至菩提。」

爾時，曼殊室利童子白佛言：「世

ZUN 尊　！　WO 我　DANG 當　SHI 誓　YU 於　XIANG 像　FA 法

ZHUAN 轉　SHI 時　，　YI 以　ZHONG 種　ZHONG 種　FANG 方　BIAN 便

，　LING 令　ZHU 諸　JING 淨　XIN 信　SHAN 善　NAN 男　ZI 子

SHAN 善　NU 女　REN 人　DENG 等　，　DE 得　WEN 聞　SHI 世

ZUN 尊　YAO 藥　SHI 師　LIU 琉　LI 璃　GUANG 光　RU 如　LAI 來

MING 名　HAO 號　，　NAI 乃　ZHI 至　SHUI 睡　ZHONG 中　，

YI 亦　YI 以　FO 佛　MING 名　JUE 覺　WU 悟　QI 其　ER 耳

。　SHI 世　ZUN 尊　！　RUO 若　YU 於　CI 此　JING 經

SHOU 受　CHI 持　DU 讀　SONG 誦　，　HUO 或　FU 復　WEI 為

TA 他　YAN 演　SHUO 說　KAI 開　SHI 示　；　RUO 若　ZI 自

SHU 書　，　RUO 若　JIAO 教　REN 人　SHU 書　；　GONG 恭

JING 敬　ZUN 尊　ZHONG 重　，　YI 以　ZHONG 種　ZHONG 種　HUA 華

香、塗香、末香、燒香、華鬘、瓔珞、幡蓋、伎樂,而為供養;以五色綵作囊盛之;掃灑淨處,敷設高座,而用安處。爾時,四大天王,與其眷屬,及餘無量百千天眾,皆詣其所,供養守護。世尊!若此經

XIANG 香、 TU 塗 XIANG 香、 MO 末 XIANG 香、

SHAO 燒 XIANG 香、 HUA 華 MAN 鬘、 YING 瓔 LUO 珞

、 FAN 幡 GAI 蓋、 JI 伎 YUE 樂, ER 而

WEI 為 GONG 供 YANG 養; YI 以 WU 五 SE 色 CAI 綵

, ZUO 作 NANG 囊 CHENG 盛 ZHI 之; SAO 掃 SA 灑

JING 淨 CHU 處, FU 敷 SHE 設 GAO 高 ZUO 座,

ER 而 YONG 用 AN 安 CHI 處。 ER 爾 SHI 時,

SI 四 DA 大 TIAN 天 WANG 王, YU 與 QI 其 JUAN 眷

SHU 屬, JI 及 YU 餘 WU 無 LIANG 量 BAI 百 QIAN 千

TIAN 天 ZHONG 眾, JIE 皆 YI 詣 QI 其 SUO 所,

GONG 供 YANG 養 SHOU 守 HU 護。

SHI 世 ZUN 尊! RUO 若 CI 此 JING 經

寶流行之處，　有能
受持，　以彼世尊藥
師琉璃光如來本願
功德，　及聞名號，
當知是處無復橫死
；亦復不為諸惡鬼
神奪其精氣；　設已
奪者，　還得如故，
身心安樂。」
　　佛告曼殊室利
：「如是！　如是！如
汝所說。　曼殊室利

！若有淨信善男子

善女人等，欲供養

彼世尊藥師琉璃光

如來者，應先造立

彼佛形像，敷清淨

座而安處之；散種

種華，燒種種香，

以種種幢幡莊嚴其

處；七日七夜受持

八分齋戒，食清淨

食，澡浴香潔，著

清淨衣，應生無垢

濁心、無怒害心，
於一切有情起利益
安樂慈悲喜捨平等
之心，鼓樂歌讚右
繞佛像。復應念彼
如來本願功德，讀
誦此經，思惟其義
，演說開示。
隨所樂求，一
切皆遂：求長壽得
長壽，求富饒得富
饒，求官位得官位

106

，求男女得男女。

若復有人，忽得惡夢，見諸惡相，或怪鳥來集，或於住處，百怪出現；此人若以眾妙資具，恭敬供養彼世尊藥師琉璃光如來者，惡夢惡相，諸不吉祥，皆悉隱沒，不能為患。

或有水、火、

刀、毒、懸險、惡象、獅子、虎、狼、熊、羆、毒蛇、惡蠍、蜈蚣、蚰蜓、蚊虻等怖；若能至心憶念彼佛，恭敬供養，一切怖畏，皆得解脫。若他國侵擾，盜賊反亂，憶念恭敬彼如來者，亦皆解脫。復次，曼殊室

108

利！若有淨信善男子善女人等，乃至盡形不事餘天，惟當一心歸佛、法、僧，受持禁戒，若五戒、十戒、菩薩四百戒、苾芻二百五十戒、苾芻尼五百戒，於所受中或有毀犯，怖墮惡趣，若能專念彼佛名號，恭敬供養者，必定不受三惡趣生。

或有女人，臨當產時，受於極苦，若能至心稱名禮讚，恭敬供養彼如來者，眾苦皆除。所生之子，身分具足，形色端正，見者歡喜，利根聰明，安隱少病，無有非人奪其精氣。」

110

爾時，世尊告阿難言：「如我稱揚彼佛世尊藥師琉璃光如來所有功德，此是諸佛甚深行處，難可解了，汝為信不？」

阿難白言：「大德世尊！我於如來所說契經，不生疑惑。所以者何？一切如來，身語意業，無不清淨。世尊！此日月輪，可令墮落；妙高山王，可使傾動，諸佛所言，無有異也。

世尊！有諸眾生，信根不具。聞說諸佛甚深行處，作是思惟；云何但念藥師琉璃光如來一佛名號，便獲爾所功德勝利？由此不信，返生毀謗；
彼於長夜，失大利
樂，墮諸惡趣，流
轉無窮。」
佛告阿難：「是
諸有情，若聞世尊
藥師琉璃光如來名
號，至心受持，不
生疑惑，墮惡趣者
，無有是處。
阿難！此是諸
佛甚深所行，難可

XIN 信	JIE 解	；	RU 汝	JIN 今	NENG 能	SHOU 受	，
DANG 當	ZHI 知	JIE 皆	SHI 是	RU 如	LAI 來	WEI 威	LI 力
。	A 阿	NAN 難	！	YI 一	QIE 切	SHENG 聲	WEN 聞
、	DU 獨	JUE 覺	、	JI 及	WEI 未	DENG 登	DI 地
ZHU 諸	PU 菩	SA 薩	DENG 等	，	JIE 皆	XI 悉	BU 不
NENG 能	RU 如	SHI 實	XIN 信	JIE 解	；	WEI 惟	CHU 除
YI 一	SHENG 生	SUO 所	XI 繫	PU 菩	SA 薩	。	
	A 阿	NAN 難	！		REN 人	SHEN 身	NAN 難
DE 得	；	YU 於	SAN 三	BAO 寶	ZHONG 中	，	XIN 信
JING 敬	ZUN 尊	ZHONG 重	，	YI 亦	NAN 難	KE 可	DE 得
，	DE 得	WEN 聞	SHI 世	ZUN 尊	YAO 藥	SHI 師	LIU 琉
LI 璃	GUANG 光	RU 如	LAI 來	MING 名	HAO 號	，	FU 復

NAN YU SHI
難　於　是　　。

　　A　NAN　　BI　YAO　SHI
　　阿　難　！　彼　藥　師

LIU　LI　GUANG　RU　LAI　　WU　LIANG
琉　璃　光　如　來　，　無　量

PU　SA　XING　　WU　LIANG　SHAN　QAIO
菩　薩　行　、　無　量　善　巧

FANG　BIAN　　WU　LAING　GUANG　DA　YUAN
方　便　、　無　量　廣　大　願

　　WO　RUO　YI　JIE　　RUO　YI
，　我　若　一　劫　，　若　一

JIE　YU　　ER　GUANG　SHUO　ZHE
劫　餘　，　而　廣　說　者　，

JIE　KE　SU　JIN　　BI　FO　XING
劫　可　速　盡　，　彼　佛　行

YUAN　　SHAN　QIAO　FANG　BIAN　　WU
願　，　善　巧　方　便　，　無

YOU　JING　YE
有　盡　也　。」

　　ER　SHI　　ZHONG　ZHONG　YOU
　　爾　時　，　眾　中　有

YI　PU　SA　MO　HE　SA　　MING
一　菩　薩　摩　訶　薩　，　名

日救脫，即從座起，偏袒右肩，右膝著地，曲躬合掌而白佛言：「大德世尊！像法轉時，有諸眾生，為種種患之所困厄，長病羸瘦，不能飲食，喉唇乾燥，見諸方暗，死相現前，父母親屬、朋友知識，啼泣圍繞。然彼自身

WO 臥　ZAI 在　BEN 本　CHU 處　，　JAIN 見　YAN 琰　MO 魔

SHI 使　，　YIN 引　QI 其　SHEN 神　SHI 識　ZHI 至　YU 於

YAN 琰　MO 魔　FA 法　WANG 王　ZHI 之　QIAN 前　；　RAN 然

ZHU 諸　YOU 有　QING 情　，　YOU 有　JU 俱　SHENG 生　SHEN 神

，　SUI 隨　QI 其　SUO 所　ZUO 作　，　RUO 若　ZUI 罪

RUO 若　FU 福　，　JIE 皆　JU 具　SHU 書　ZHI 之　，

JIN 盡　CHI 持　SHOU 授　YU 與　YAN 琰　MO 魔　FA 法　WANG 王

。　ER 爾　SHI 時　，　BI 彼　WANG 王　TUI 推　WEN 問

QI 其　REN 人　，　JI 計　SUAN 算　SUO 所　ZUO 作　，

SUI 隨　QI 其　ZUI 罪　FU 福　，　ER 而　CHU 處　DUAN 斷

ZHI 之　。

SHI 時　BI 彼　BING 病　REN 人　QIN 親　SHU 屬

臥在本處，見琰魔使，引其神識至於琰魔法王之前；然諸有情，有俱生神，隨其所作，若罪若福，皆具書之，持授與琰魔法王。爾時，彼王推問其人，計算所作，隨其罪福，而處斷之。時彼病人親屬

、知識，若能為彼歸依世尊藥師琉璃光如來，請諸眾僧轉讀此經，然七層之燈，懸五色續命神幡，或有是處，彼識得還。如在夢中，明了自見。或經七日，或二十一日，或三十五日，或四十九日，彼識還時，

RU 如 CONG 從 MENG 夢 JUE 覺 ， JIE 皆 ZI 自 YI 憶

ZHI 知 SHAN 善 BU 不 SHAN 善 YE 業 SUO 所 DE 得 GUO 果

BAO 報 。 YOU 由 ZI 自 ZHENG 證 JIAN 見 YE 業 GUO 果

BAO 報 GU 故 ， NAI 乃 ZHI 至 MING 命 NAN 難 ，

YI 亦 BU 不 ZAO 造 ZUO 作 ZHU 諸 E 惡 ZHI 之 YE 業

。

SHI 是 GU 故 ， JING 淨 XIN 信 SHAN 善

NAN 男 ZI 子 SHAN 善 NU 女 REN 人 DENG 等 ， JIE 皆

YING 應 SHOU 受 CHI 持 YAO 藥 SHI 師 LIU 琉 LI 璃 GUANG 光

RU 如 LAI 來 MING 名 HAO 號 。 SUI 隨 LI 力 SUO 所

NENG 能 ， GONG 恭 JING 敬 GONG 供 YANG 養 。」

ER 爾 SHI 時 ， A 阿 NAN 難 WEN 問

救脫菩薩言：「善男子！應云何恭敬供養彼世尊藥師琉璃光如來？續命幡燈，復云何造？」

救脫菩薩言：「大德！若有病人，欲脫病苦，當為其人，七日七夜受持八分齋戒，應以飲食及餘資具，隨力所辦，供養苾芻僧

; ZHOU 晝　YE 夜　LIU 六　SHI 時　, 　LI 禮　BAI 拜

GONG 供　YANG 養　BI 彼　SHI 世　ZUN 尊　YAO 藥　SHI 師　LIU 琉

LI 璃　GUANG 光　RU 如　LAI 來　, 　DU 讀　SONG 誦　CI 此

JING 經　SI 四　SHI 十　JIU 九　BIAN 遍　, 　RAN 燃　SI 四

SHI 十　JIU 九　DENG 燈　, 　ZAO 造　BI 彼　RU 如　LAI 來

XING 形　XIANG 像　QI 七　QU 軀　, 　YI 一　YI 一　XIANG 像

QIAN 前　, 　GE 各　ZHI 置　QI 七　DENG 燈　, 　YI 一

YI 一　DENG 燈　LIANG 量　, 　DA 大　RU 如　CHE 車　LUN 輪

, 　NAI 乃　ZHI 至　SI 四　SHI 十　JIU 九　RI 日　GUANG 光

MING 明　BU 不　JUE 絕　; 　ZAO 造　WU 五　SE 色　CAI 綵

FAN 幡　, 　CHANG 長　SI 四　SHI 十　JIU 九　ZE 搩　SHOU 手

; 　YING 應　FANG 放　ZA 雜　LEI 類　ZHONG 眾　SHENG 生　ZHI 至

121

四十九；可得過度
SI SHI JIU ; KE DE GUO DU

危厄之難，不為諸
WEI E ZHI NAN , BU WEI ZHU

橫惡鬼所持。
HENG E GUI SUO CHI 。

復次，阿難！
FU CI , A NAN !

若剎帝利、灌頂王
RUO CHA DI LI 、 GUAN DING WANG

等，災難起時，所
DENG , ZAI NAN QI SHI , SUO

謂人眾疾疫難、他
WEI REN ZHONG JI YI NAN 、 TA

國侵逼難、自界叛
GUO QIN BI NAN 、 ZI JIE PAN

逆難、星宿變怪難
NI NAN 、 XING SU BIAN GUAI NAN

、日月薄蝕難、非
、 RI YUE BAO SHI NAN 、 FEI

時風雨難，彼剎帝
SHI FENG YU NAN , BI CHA DI

利、灌頂王等，爾
LI 、 GUAN DING WANG DENG , ER

SHI YING YU YI QIE YOU QING ，
時　應　於　一　切　有　情

QI CI BEI XIN ， SHE ZHU XI
起　慈　悲　心　，　赦　諸　繫

BI ； YI QIAN SUO SHUO GONG YANG
閉　；　依　前　所　說　供　養

ZHI FA ， GONG YANG BI SHI ZUN
之　法　，　供　養　彼　世　尊

YAO SHI LIU LI GUANG RU LAI 。
藥　師　琉　璃　光　如　來　。

YOU CI SHAN GEN ， JI BI RU
由　此　善　根　，　及　彼　如

LAI BEN YUAN LI GU ， LING QI
來　本　願　力　故　，　令　其

GUO JIE ， JI DE AN YIN ，
國　界　，　即　得　安　隱　，

FENG YU SHUN SHI ， GU JIA CHENG
風　雨　順　時　，　穀　稼　成

SHOU ； YI QIE YOU QING ， WU
熟　；　一　切　有　情　，　無

BING HUAN LE ； YU QI GUO ZHONG
病　歡　樂　；　於　其　國　中

， WU YOU BAO E YAO CHA DENG
，　無　有　暴　惡　藥　叉　等

神，惱有情者；一切惡相，皆即隱沒；而剎帝利、灌頂王等，壽命色力，無病自在，皆得增益。

阿難！若帝后、妃主、儲君、王子、大臣、輔相、中宮、綵女、百官、黎庶，為病所苦，及餘厄難，亦應

124

造立五色神幡，燃燈續明，放諸生命，散雜色華，燒眾名香，病得除愈，眾難解脫。」

爾時，阿難問救脫菩薩言：「善男子！云何已盡之命而可增益？」

救脫菩薩言：

「大德！汝豈不聞如來說，有九橫死耶

125

？是故勸造續命幡燈，修諸福德；以修福故，盡其壽命，不經苦患。」

阿難問言：「九橫云何？」

救脫菩薩言：

「若諸有情，得病雖輕，然無醫藥及看病者；設復遇醫，授以非藥，實不應死，而便橫死。又，信世間邪魔、外道、妖孽之師，妄說禍福，便生恐動，心不自正，卜問覓禍，殺種種眾生，解奏神明，呼諸魍魎，請乞福祐，欲冀延年，終不能得。愚癡迷惑，信邪倒見，遂令橫死，入於地獄，無有出期，是名初橫。

二者，橫被王法之所誅戮。三者，畋獵嬉戲，耽淫嗜酒，放逸無度，橫為非人奪其精氣。四者，橫為火焚。五者，橫為水溺。六者，橫為種種惡獸所噉。七者，橫墮山崖。八者，橫為毒藥、厭禱、咒詛、起屍鬼等之

SUO ZHONG HAI JIU ZHE JI
所　中　害　。　九　者　，　飢

KE SUO KUN BU DE YIN SHI
渴　所　困　，　不　得　飲　食

ER BIAN HENG SI SHI WEI
，　而　便　橫　死　。　是　為

RU LAI LUE SHUO HENG SI YOU
如　來　略　說　橫　死　，　有

CI JIU ZHONG JI YU FU YOU
此　九　種　。　其　餘　復　有

WU LIANG ZHU HENG NAN KE JU
無　量　諸　橫　，　難　可　具

SHUO
說　。

FU CI A NAN
　　復　次　，　阿　難　，

BI YAN MO WANG ZHU LING SHI JIAN
彼　琰　魔　王　主　領　世　間

MING JI ZHI JI RUO ZHU YOU
名　籍　之　記　，　若　諸　有

QING BU XIAO WU NI PO
情　，　不　孝　五　逆　，　破

RU SAN BAO HUAI JUN CHEN FA
辱　三　寶　，　壞　君　臣　法

HUI	YU	XING	JIE		YAN	MO	FA
毀	於	信	戒	。	琰	魔	法

WANG		SUI	ZUI	QING	ZHONG	KAO	ER
王	，	隨	罪	輕	重	考	而

FA	ZHI		SHI	GU	WO	JIN	QUAN
罰	之	。	是	故	我	今	勸

ZHU	YOU	QING		RAN	DENG	ZAO	FAN
諸	有	情	，	燃	燈	造	幡

FANG	SHENG	XIU	FU		LING	DU	KU
放	生	修	福	，	令	度	苦

E		BU	ZAO	ZHONG	NAN		
厄	，	不	遭	眾	難	。」	

	ER	SHI		ZHONG	ZHONG	YOU	
	爾	時	，	眾	中	有	

SHI	ER	YAO	CHA	DA	JIANG		JU
十	二	藥	叉	大	將	，	俱

ZAI	HUI	ZUO		SUO	WEI		GONG
在	會	座	，	所	謂	：	宮

PI	LUO	DA	JIANG		FA	ZHE	LUO
毘	羅	大	將	、	伐	折	羅

DA	JIANG		MI	QI	LUO	DA	JIANG
大	將	、	迷	企	羅	大	將

	AN	DI	LUO	DA	JIANG		E
、	安	底	羅	大	將	、	額

彌羅大將、珊底羅大將、因達羅大將、波夷羅大將、摩虎羅大將、真達羅大將、招杜羅大將、毘羯羅大將。此十二藥叉大將，一一各有七千藥叉，以為眷屬，同時舉聲白佛言：「世尊！我等今者，蒙佛威力，得聞世

尊藥師琉璃光如來
名號，不復更有惡
趣之怖。我等相率
，皆同一心，乃至
盡形，歸佛、法、
僧，誓當荷負一切
有情，為作義利饒
益安樂。隨於何等
村城國邑，空閒林
中，若有流布此經
，或復受持藥師琉
璃光如來名號恭敬

GONG YANG ZHE， WO DENG JUAN SHU
供 養 者 ， 我 等 眷 屬

， WEI HU SHI REN ， JIE SHI
， 衛 護 是 人 ， 皆 使

JIE TUO YI QIE KU NAN ； ZHU
解 脫 一 切 苦 難 ； 諸

YOU YUAN QIU， XI LING MAN ZU
有 願 求 ， 悉 令 滿 足

。 HUO YOU JI E QIU DU TUO
。 或 有 疾 厄 求 度 脫

ZHE， YI YING DU SONG CI JING
者 ， 亦 應 讀 誦 此 經

， YI WU SE LU， JIE WO
， 以 五 色 縷 ， 結 我

MING ZI， DE RU YUAN YI，
名 字 ， 得 如 願 已 ，

RAN HOU JIE JIE。」
然 後 解 結 。」

ER SHI， SHI ZUN ZAN
爾 時 ， 世 尊 讚

ZHU YAO CHA DA JIANG YAN :「SHAN
諸 藥 叉 大 將 言 :「善

ZAI！ SHAN ZAI！ DA YAO CHA
哉 ！ 善 哉 ！ 大 藥 叉

將！汝等念報世尊
藥師琉璃光如來恩
德者，常應如是利
益安樂一切有情。」

爾時，阿難白佛言：「世尊！當何名此法門？我等云何奉持？」

佛告阿難：「此法門名說藥師琉璃光如來本願功德，

YI	MING	SHUO	SHI	ER	SHEN	JIANG	RAO
亦	名	說	十	二	神	將	饒
YI	YOU	QING	JIE	YUAN	SHEN	ZHOU	，
益	有	情	結	願	神	咒	，
YI	MING	BA	CHU	YI	QIE	YE	ZHANG
亦	名	拔	除	一	切	業	障
；	YING	RU	SHI	CHI			
；	應	如	是	持。」			
	SHI	BAO	QIE	FAN	SHUO	SHI	YU
	時	薄	伽	梵	說	是	語
YI		ZHU	PU	SA	MO	HE	SA
已	，	諸	菩	薩	摩	訶	薩
JI	DA	SHENG	WEN		GUO	WANG	
及	大	聲	聞	、	國	王	、
DA	CHEN		PO	LUO	MEN		JU
大	臣	、	婆	羅	門	、	居
SHI		TIAN		LONG		YAO	CHA
士	、	天	、	龍	、	藥	叉
	JIAN	DA	FU		A	SU	LUO
、	健	達	縛	、	阿	素	洛
	JIE	LU	TU		JIN	NA	LUO
、	揭	路	茶	、	緊	捺	洛
	MO	HU	LUO	QIE		REN	FEI
、	莫	呼	洛	伽	、	人	非

REN DENG ， YI QIE DA ZHONG ，
人 等 ， 一 切 大 眾 ，

WEN FO SUO SHUO ， JIE DA HUAN
聞 佛 所 說 ， 皆 大 歡

XI ， XIN SHOU FENG XING 。
喜 ， 信 受 奉 行 。

YAO SHI LIU LI GUANG RU LAI BEN
藥 師 琉 璃 光 如 來 本

YUAN GONG DE JING
願 功 德 經

YAO SHI GUAN DING ZHEN YAN
藥 師 灌 頂 真 言

NAN 南	MO 無	BAO 薄	QIE 伽	FA 伐	DI 帝	，	BI 鞞
SHA 殺	SHE 社	，	JU 窶	LU 嚕	BI 薛	LIU 琉	LI 璃
，	BO 缽	LA 喇	PO 婆	，	HE 喝	LUO 囉	SHE 闍
YE 也	，	DA 怛	TUO 陀	JIE 揭	DUO 多	YE 耶	，
A 阿	LUO 囉	HE 喝	DI 帝	，	SAN 三	MIAO 藐	SAN 三
BO 勃	TUO 陀	YE 耶	，	DA 怛	ZHI 姪	TUO 陀	。
AN 唵	！	BI 鞞	SHA 殺	SHI 逝	，	BI 鞞	SHA 殺
SHI 逝	，	BI 鞞	SHA 殺	SHE 社	！	SAN 三	MO 沒
JIE 揭	DI 帝	SHA 莎	HE 訶	！			

BAI YUAN
拜 願

NAN 南	MO 無	XIAO 消	ZAI 災	YAN 延	SHOU 壽	YAO 藥	SHI 師	FO 佛

SAN GUI YI
三 皈 依

ZI	GUI	YI	FO	DANG	YUAN	ZHONG	SHENG
自	皈	依	佛	當	願	眾	生
TI	JIE	DA	DAO	FA	WU	SHANG	XIN
體	解	大	道	發	無	上	心
ZI	GUI	YI	FA	DANG	YUAN	ZHONG	SHENG
自	皈	依	法	當	願	眾	生
SHEN	RU	JING	ZANG	ZHI	HUI	RU	HAI
深	入	經	藏	智	慧	如	海
ZI	GUI	YI	SENG	DANG	YUAN	ZHONG	SHENG
自	皈	依	僧	當	願	眾	生
TONG	LI	DA	ZHONG	YI	QIE	WU	AI
統	理	大	眾	一	切	無	礙

HUI XIANG
迴 向

CI	BEI	XI	SHE	BIAN	FA	JIE
慈	悲	喜	捨	遍	法	界
XI	FU	JIE	YUAN	LI	REN	TIAN
惜	福	結	緣	利	人	天
CHAN	JING	JIE	HEN	PING	DENG	REN
禪	淨	戒	行	平	等	忍
CAN	KUI	GAN	EN	DA	YUAN	XIN
慚	愧	感	恩	大	願	心

Prayer and Vows Generated in the Medicine Buddha Dharma Service

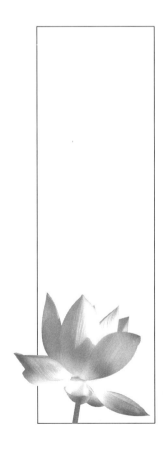

Prayer and Vows Generated in the Medicine Buddha Dharma Service

Our respected Medicine Buddha:

In this Medicine Buddha Dharma Assembly, we recite the sutra, chant your title, bow to your sacred image, light lamps, and share resources such as food and clothing with people who are in need. Now, we have some heart-felt wishes to express to you:

First of all, we will definitely follow your instructions, generating great and pristine vows:

We will follow your first vow:
Seeing all sentient beings in the world as equal and free as all Buddhas.

We will follow your second vow:
May whatever we engage in be of benefit to others.

We will follow your third vow:
May all nurturing resources be accessible and abundant to all sentient beings.

We will follow your fourth vow:
May all sentient beings stay clear of heretical practice and instead abide in bodhi. May everyone recognize the truth of cause and effect, follow the teaching of the Mahayana, and share a civilized life of correct view and correct understanding.

We will follow your fifth vow:
May we uphold the precepts completely, without flaw. If our conduct strays from the path of virtue presented in these precepts, may you help us return to their pristine nature.

We will follow your sixth vow:
May all sentient beings who suffer from illness or defective fac-

ulties return to full functioning and gain both pleasant countenances and intuitive mastery of all knowledge and skills.

We will follow your seventh vow:

May all sentient beings who are sick and poor gain blessings from your magnificent power so that all their illnesses shall be eliminated and they can enjoy peace and joy of body and mind.

We will follow your eighth vow:

May any man who would like to become a woman in his next life be born with all the pleasant features of a woman. If there is any woman who is weary of the disadvantages of being female, as she wishes, she shall be reborn as a man with characteristics of a true man in her next life.

We will follow your ninth vow:

May those sentient beings who engage in heretical practice take leave of their harmful friends and vicious environment, free themselves from all entanglements, and return to the straight path of truth.

We will follow your tenth vow:

May any individual who is unjustly imprisoned gain justice. Even if there is no injustice involved, may his/her sentence be commuted and he/she be given another chance to restore his/her uprightness.

We will follow your eleventh vow:

May all sentient beings that lack food and clothing obtain delicate clothing and exquisite food. Whatever resource they desire shall be available to them.

We will follow your twelfth vow:

May all sentient beings that have experienced insults, invasions from others, or racial discrimination be treated with respect and equality.

Secondly, we will definitely follow your instructions,

praying that the Buddha, the Dharma, and the Sangha might strengthen our moral capacity so that we can help eliminate all disasters in the world:

We pray for the benefit of all sentient beings in the world that there be no damage due to floods.

We pray for the benefit of all sentient beings in the world that there be no wounding or disabling due to fights and wars.

We pray for the benefit of all sentient beings in the world that there be no racial discrimination.

We pray for the benefit of all sentient beings in the world that there be no violence in society.

We pray for the benefit of all sentient beings in the world that there be no worry due to economic crisis or depression.

We pray for the benefit of all sentient beings in the world that there be no political persecution.

We pray for the benefit of all sentient beings in the world that there be no ill will or slander.

We pray for the benefit of all sentient beings in the world that there be no disharmony between self and others.

We pray for the benefit of all sentient beings in the world that there be no agitation and anxiety.

We pray for the benefit of all sentient beings in the world that there be no damage due to earthquakes.

We pray for the benefit of all sentient beings in the world that there be no grief due to being physically deformed or disabled.

We pray for the benefit of all sentient beings in the world that there be no trauma due to unwilling separation between loved ones, while living or dying.

Thirdly, we will definitely follow your instructions and advocate your spirit of releasing those who are suffering:

Using our best efforts, we will offer medication to those who suffer from illness and help them regain health.

Using our best efforts, we will give food to those who suffer from hunger and help them experience satisfaction.

Using our best efforts, we will give clothing to those who lack clothing and help them to remain warm and comfortable.

Using our best efforts, we will speak benevolent words to those who are suffering such that they might feel comfort and joy.

Using our best efforts, we will lend a hand to those who are suffering such that they might proceed smoothly.

Using our best efforts, we will share joy with those who are suffering such that they might be happy as well.

Using our best efforts, we will share the teachings of fearlessness with those who are suffering such that they might feel safe and secure.

Using our best efforts, we will give shelters to those who do not have a place to live such that they might settle their bodies.

Using our best efforts, we will treat those who are suffering with respect such that they might have self-esteem and treat themselves with love.

Using our best efforts, we will rebuild the confidence of those who are suffering such that they might be prosperous again.

Using our best efforts, we will help those who are suffering to feel love such that they might experience peace and joy.

Using our best efforts, we will share the Dharma with those who are suffering such that they might liberate themselves.

Fourthly, we will definitely follow your instructions, and maintain and abide the infinite life of all sentient beings:

We pray that all sentient beings in the world shall maintain and abide the infinite life of Buddhahood from their physical form.

We pray that all sentient beings in the world shall maintain and abide the infinite life of spirituality.

We pray that all sentient beings in the world shall maintain and abide the infinite life of wisdom.

We pray that all sentient beings in the world shall maintain and abide the infinite life of meritorious virtues.

We pray that all sentient beings in the world shall maintain and abide the infinite life of speech and words.

We pray that all sentient beings in the world shall maintain and abide the infinite life of society.

We pray that all sentient beings in the world shall maintain and abide the infinite life of their family and relatives.

We pray that all sentient beings in the world shall maintain and abide the infinite life of beauty and health.

We pray that all sentient beings in the world shall maintain and abide the infinite life of honor.

We pray that all sentient beings in the world shall maintain and abide the infinite life of inner strength.

We pray that all sentient beings in the world shall maintain and abide the infinite life of faith.

We pray that all sentient beings in the world shall maintain and abide the infinite life of awakening.

Fifthly, we will definitely follow your instructions, lighting up the lamp within our being:

Lighting up our innate lamp of prajna wisdom.

Lighting up our innate lamp of compassion and skillful means.

Lighting up our innate lamp of prosperity and peace.

Lighting up our innate lamp of correct view and correct understanding.

Lighting up our innate lamp of Dharma joy and Chan ease.

Lighting up our innate lamp of pristine precepts.

Lighting up our innate lamp of supporting the Dharma and the temple.

Lighting up our innate lamp of respect for the Triple Gem.

Lighting up our innate lamp of diligence.

Lighting up our innate lamp of enlightened supreme awareness.   .

Lighting up our innate lamp of constantly present perfection.

Lighting up our innate lamp that radiates Buddha's light universally.

Our respected Medicine Buddha:

With my bow, I make an offering of my body to you.

With praises, I make an offering of my speech to you.

Taking refuge in you, I make an offering of my mind.

With my pristine body, speech, and mind, I request that you permeate the Dharma realm with your magnificent virtues and bring our vows to fruition.

Once again, I sincerely make two bows before you.

Buddhism, Medicine, and Health

Buddhism, Medicine, and Health

Introduction

Since the origin of the world, birth, aging, illness, and death have been unavoidable. Prince Siddhartha learned of this truth when he ventured beyond his palace and visited the poor area of town. Here, amidst beggars, sick people, and decrepit elders, he saw the reality of life. Immediately, a desire arose in his heart to relieve the pain and suffering of these people. Thus, he renounced his life of luxury and became a monk, hoping that through meditation and cultivation he could find solutions for the poor and ailing people.

From the beginning, the Buddha (formerly Prince Siddhartha) realized that just as one can suffer from physical disease, one could also suffer from an unhealthy mindset. To cure both diseases of the body and mind, the Buddha devoted his entire life to passing down the knowledge of the Tripitaka.[1] While the Buddha sought to cure both physical and mental illness, emphasis was placed upon the mind. He used the knowledge of the Dharma to heal the illness that arose from the three poisons: greed, anger, and ignorance. The Buddha's medicine treats disease starting from the patients' minds, curing them of the three poisons. Psychologists also treat illness by working with their patient's mental state, but this is quite different from the Buddhist practice of treating the mind. According to Buddhism, the pure and wondrous Dharma is the perfect medication for an ailing mind, as well as a sick body.

Keeping both the mind and body healthy is important, for the body is the vehicle in which we can practice the Dharma. Like all things, the mind and the body are interdependent; the health of the mind influences the health of the body, and vice versa — the health of the body influences the health of the mind. With a healthy body as a tool, we can cultivate a compassionate heart and a clear mind. With a cultivated mind, we are able to examine ourselves, clearly see the nature of our problems, and then work to resolve them. We will then be approaching the path to true health.

Buddhism and Medical Science

In the sutras, we can find analogies that describe the Buddha as the doctor, knowledge of the Dharma as the medicine, monastics as the nursing staff, and all people as the patients. According to this medical analogy, Buddhism is considered a medication with a broad meaning — a medication that can cure the ailments in all aspects of life. In general, but with exceptions, Western medicine functions within a much smaller framework. Western medicine typically approaches illness through physical symptoms. This approach tends to temporarily reduce the suffering and remove the symptoms for a period, but a lack of symptoms does not mean that the root cause has been identified and removed. Therefore, the complete elimination of the disease has not occurred. Buddhism offers patients not only symptomatic relief, but also spiritual guidance to ensure overall and long-lasting health.

While Western researchers have conducted massive studies on pathology, pharmacology, immunology, and anatomy, enabling them to develop more sophisticated medical techniques, scientists still doubt that religion can help explain the cause of a disease. Without validating the role of religion in disease, scientists remain quite distant from the definition of disease, its causes, and its treatments as understood from a religious perspective. According to Buddhism, it is not enough to approach medicine in a manner that simply eradicates symptoms; the spiritual aspect of disease and its mind-based causes and remedies must be the primary consideration.

Only recently have science and religion started to communicate and blend in a manner that is beginning to narrow the gap between a scientific approach to disease and one rooted in religion. For instance, the U.S. government coordinated international conferences on "The Relationship Between Religion and Health." Also, Harvard Medical School offers a class entitled "The Essence of Medicine." Religion is gradually influencing the biological, psychological, and social medicine of Western society. Buddhism has played a significant role in uniting spirituality and medicine in the West.

In the East, religion has impacted the field of health and medicine for a much longer time. Eastern medical practitioners never doubted the role of religion in disease; the two have been integrated for thousands of years. Out of thousands of documents in the Tripitaka, a significant number contain records about Buddhist medicine. When this canon of discourses and sutras was brought to China, the most salient aspects of Indian Buddhism blended with the most highly regarded aspects of Chinese medicine. Through modifications and improvements contributed by numerous Buddhist masters from the past and present, the Chinese Buddhist medical system has evolved into the one that presently exists. In the following pages, I will elaborate further on the Buddhist understanding of illness and disease and the Buddhist approach to medicine and healing.

Buddha as the Great Doctor

When the Buddha was young, he learned the science of medicine.[2] He became very knowledgeable about the nature and cure of diseases. According to the sutras, a famous physician named Jivaka further advanced his medical practice and mastered additional skills by learning from the Buddha and following the Buddha's instructions. Jivaka performed several remarkable surgical procedures, earning a respectable reputation in the medical field. One of his well-known operations involved the repair of an obstructed colon. Jivaka performed this surgery using a sequence of techniques similar to contemporary practices: administering anesthesia, opening the abdominal region, repairing the colon, and finally, closing the incision with stitches. Though a trained physician, Jivaka became even more competent in his mastery of medicine under the Buddha's spiritual and medical guidance.

In addition to records about the Buddha and Jivaka, numerous sutras such as the *Sutra of Buddha's Diagnosis*, the *Sutra of the Buddha as a Great Doctor*, the *Sutra on Relieving Piles,* the *Sutra on Healing Mental Distractions of Improper Meditation*, the *Sutra of Healing Dental Diseases,* the *Sutra of Dharani for Healing All Diseases,* the *Sutra of Dharani for Season's Diseases,* the *Sutra of Golden Light (Suvarnaprabhasottama Sutra)*, the *Five Part Vinaya*, the *Four Part Vinaya, Ten Recitations Vinaya*, and *Great Compilation of Monastic Rules (Mahasanghavinaya)* contain many other references to the Buddha's knowledge about medicine. The Buddha truly deserves to be regarded as the grand patriarch of Buddhist medicine. He was capable of curing diseases not only of the body but also of the mind, which were his specialty. Today, when a patient seeks a physician's care for a physical ailment, the physician typically only pays attention to the painful symptoms in the body, ignoring both the causes and the suffering in the mind. By not investigating and discovering the true roots of the disease, they only accomplish a fraction of real healing. They do very little to heal the patients' unhappiness, for they do not recognize and understand the true cause of the human life cycle of birth, aging, illness, and death. They do not take into account that karma and mental constructs have something to do with the origins of illness.

The Buddha's realization of what induces the perpetual cycle of rebirth and the stages of aging, illness, and death enabled him to guide others to live with ultimate physical and mental health. The Buddha eliminated disease by going to the heart of the cause and drawing upon his knowledge of the proper remedy. In the *Gradual Discourses of the Buddha* (*Anguttara-nikaya*), the Buddha explained that an imbalance of *chi* (*qi*),[3] an overabundance of phlegm, and an increase or decrease in the body's temperature could be treated with clarified butter, honey, and oil-based food respectively.

Regarding mental health, greed, anger, and ignorance are understood as the three gravest psychological diseases. The Buddha taught that greed could be cured by the contemplation of impurity, anger by the contemplation and practice of kindness, and ignorance by the contemplation of the true nature of all things and the cultivation of wisdom. These are the medications that the Buddha encouraged everyone to use in order to heal the diseases of both body and mind.

In the *Sutra of Buddha's Diagnosis*, the Buddha explained that a doctor should progress through four steps when helping a patient. Doctors must: 1) discover the origin of the illness, 2) achieve a thorough understanding of the illness, 3) prescribe the appropriate medication to cure the illness, and 4) completely cure the illness in a manner that prevents it from reoccurring. In addition to mastering these four criteria, a good doctor should always act with a generous heart when treating patients, considering them as his or her dearest friends.

The Buddha also identified five important practices for caretakers — nurses, family members, friends, and others — to be aware of as they cared for patients. He encouraged caretakers to: 1) insure that the patients are tended to by good-hearted and skillful doctors, 2) wake up earlier and go to bed later than patients and always remain alert to the patient's needs, 3) speak to their patients in a kind and compassionate voice when they are feeling depressed or uneasy, 4) nourish the patients with the proper food in the correct amounts and intervals according to the nature of the ailment and according to the doctor's instructions, and 5) talk with skill and ease about the Dharma with the patients; instructing them in proper healthcare for the body and mind.

Lastly, the Buddha offered advice to patients in order to help them heal quickly and thoroughly. He recommended that patients: 1) be cautious and selective about the food they eat, 2) consume food at the proper intervals, 3) stay in touch with their doctors and nurses and always act kindly and graciously towards them, 4) keep an optimistic or hopeful outlook, and 5) be kind and considerate of those who are caring for you. The Buddha believed that a cooperative effort from the doctors, caretakers, and patients yielded the best results from treatment. The Buddha was not just an average doctor; he was an exceptional doctor who had vision and insight.

Medical Theories in Buddhism

According to Chinese medicine, diseases are caused by seven internal and six external elements. The internal elements are extreme levels of happiness, anger, anxiety, a ruminating mind, sadness, fear, and shock. The external elements are coldness, summer-heat, dryness, heat, dampness, and wind. The seven internal elements, also referred to as emotions, are believed to cause illness because they directly impair the healthy functioning of the five main organs of human beings. Extreme levels of either happiness or fear damage the heart, anger harms the liver, anxiety harms the lungs, a ruminating mind affects the spleen, and shock hurts the kidneys. According to Chinese medicine, a healthy and balanced emotional life is essential in maintaining one's physical health.

Various Buddhist sutras describe the causes of disease in a similar manner. For example, the *Sutra of Buddha's Diagnosis* mentions that there are ten causes and conditions of sickness. These reasons are: 1) sitting for too long a period without moving, 2) eating too much, 3) sadness, 4) fatigue, 5) excessive sexual desire, 6) anger, 7) postponing excrement, 8) postponing urination, 9) holding the breath, and 10) suppressing gas. Approaching the causes of disease from a slightly different angle, the *Great Techniques of Stopping* [*Delusion*] *and Seeing* [*Truth*] points out six origins for disease. They are described as: 1) an imbalance of the four elements (earth, water, fire, and wind), 2) irregular dietary habits, 3) incorrect meditation methods, 4) disturbances by spirits, 5) demon possession, and 6) the force of bad karma. Illness that originates from most of these origins can be cured if people improve their diet, become more aware of their bodies' natural processes, and get plenty of rest. However, the last three causes, 4) - 6), are related to karma, and one must work on improving his/her character and purifying his/her mind in order to be cured. A person afflicted for the last three reasons needs to spend time in spiritual practice, repentance, and doing good deeds. Only then will his/her illness begin to go away. The *Treatise on Perfection of Great Wisdom* (*Mahaprajnaparamita Sastra*) states that illness is caused either by internal or external causes and conditions. Still, the *Path of Purification* (*Visuddhimagga*) mentions additional causes of disease, but they are too numerous to list here. All of the theories on the various causes of illness can be grouped into two main categories: A) the imbalance of the four elements and B) the presence of the three poisons of greed, anger, and ignorance. The following is a detailed discussion of these two classifications.

A. The Imbalance of the Four Elements

According to Buddhism, the body is composed of four impermanent elements — earth, water, fire, and wind. Only consciousness is reborn in one of the six realms. This theory is the foundation of Indian Buddhist medical science. Chinese medicine believes the body to be comprised of a unique system of subsidiary channels that transmits vital energy (chi), blood, nutrients, and other substances through the five organs and six internal regions in one's body. When this intricate circulation system is flowing properly, the four elements stay in balance, the major organs can perform their essential functions, and the body remains healthy.

The *Condensed Techniques of Stopping* [*Delusion*] *and Seeing* [*Truth*] states that each of the four elements is able to cause one hundred and one diseases, with a total of four hundred and four diseases possible. Each element is connected to certain types of disease. For instance, the earth element is related to diseases that make the body become heavy, stiff, and painful, such as arthritis; the water element afflicts the body with diarrhea, stomachaches, and difficult digestion; the fire element causes fever, constipation, and problems urinating; lastly, the wind element is related to breathing difficulties and vomiting.

The third volume of *Nanhai Ji Gui Neifa Zhuan* states that, "If diseases are related to the four elements, they are usually caused by overeating or overexertion." An imbalance of the four elements and the resulting illness can also occur due to a diet that is not in tune with the four seasons. When the seasons change and the temperature varies from cool to cold to warm to hot, it is important to adjust our diet in a manner that enables the body to function at its best. In the *Sutra of Golden Light*, a young man asked his father who was a doctor, "How do we cure the suffering of human beings and cure diseases that arise from an imbalance of the four elements?" The doctor responded to his son by saying, "We live our lives through four seasons of three months, or six seasons of two months in some parts of the world. Whether four or six, we must live according to the seasons, eating food that corresponds with hot and cold, warm and cool. In this way, our bodies will benefit. A good doctor is well learned in prescribing the right food and medicine to adjust the four elements and nourish a patient's body during a particular season. When the season and the food are in balance, so too will the body be in balance."

Eating a reasonable amount and adjusting what we eat according to seasonal changes are two important factors in maintaining balance among the four elements and allowing chi to circulate unimpeded through our bodies. We automatically dress differently when the seasons change in order to comfort and protect ourselves during a particular temperature change or altered weather conditions. If we adopt this practice and adjust our diet with the weather and seasons, we help our bodies to stay balanced and guard against disease.

B. Greed, Anger, and Ignorance

Greed, anger, and ignorance, sometimes referred to as "the three poisons," are also reasons why people are afflicted with sickness. When one is stuck in any one of these destructive mental states, one opens the door and invites disease. The *Vimalakirti Sutra* states, "All the diseases I have right now are derived from illusory thoughts I have had in the past ... because human beings are attached to a 'self,' afflictions and diseases have the chance to be born in their bodies." When one allows oneself to be ruled by the three poisons, the psychological and physical health hazards are numerous and can be quite debilitating. The following descriptions provide insight into how greed, anger, and ignorance cause illness:

1. Greed

Greed is defined as an improper and excessive desire for something. For example, one is more likely to overeat when one is having a favorite meal. Such greed can then lead to an overly full stomach and the food will not be well digested. Or, one may like food so much that he/she eats much too frequently. This type of desire, which cannot be satisfied, can cause obesity, fatigue, and heart problems. Greed is never without consequences.

People can also have excessive desires for sensory experience. In the *Interpretation of Great Techniques of Stopping [Delusion] and Seeing [Truth]*, it is stated that too much attachment to what we perceive through sound, smell, sight, taste, and touch can cause both psychological and physical illness. A person may cling to the experience of these five sensations, which can cause an imbalance in one's rational thoughts and disturb one's ability to make moral choices. Physical health problems can also arise. In the Buddhist health theory, those who are too attached to physical appearance will suffer from diseases of the liver. Those who are too attached to sounds will suffer from kidney diseases. Those who are too attached to aromas will suffer from lung diseases. Those who are too attached to taste will suffer from heart diseases. And those who are too attached to the sensation of touch will suffer from spleen diseases. Thus, when we encounter the multitude of sensations that are a natural part of daily life, it is best to maintain a balanced attitude and practice the Middle Way.[4] In order to maintain optimum physical and mental health, the Middle Way is also the best way to approach sleeping, eating, and exercising. When one sleeps too much, one will not have a clear mind. When one eats too much food that is high in cholesterol and sugar, one is gradually increasing the risk of poor health and could ultimately face chronic disease, such as diabetes or heart disease. In today's fast-paced society that promotes working excessively and watching hours of television, people do not exercise enough, and eventually, this has an adverse affect on their bodies. Additionally, nowadays people are constantly exposed to a noisy and stressful environment, which can cause people to become sick more easily. If one decreases one's greed and desire and approaches life with the attitude of the Middle Path, one can lead a healthier life.

2. Anger

The fourteenth volume of the *Treatise on Perfection of Great Wisdom* states that, "Anger is the most toxic emotion compared to the other two poisons; its harm far exceeds all of the other afflictions as well. Of the ninety-eight torments,[5] anger is the hardest one to subdue; among all psychological problems, anger is the most difficult to cure." Although anger is a psychological problem, it can also lead to severe physical consequences. For example, when aversion and anger arise in a person, the blood vessels become constricted, causing a rise in blood pressure and thus increasing the risk of a heart attack.

In writing about anger, Venerable Punengsong from the Qing Dynasty tells us,

A good doctor always finds out
  The cause of a sickness first.
  Anger is quite harmful
  To someone who is sick.
The relationship between a patient's pulse
  And his illness is delicate.
With the correct prescription,
  We can heal ourselves of our illness.

As doctors examine their patients to determine the cause of illness and the proper medication to prescribe, one of the most essential ingredients of treatment is pacifying the patients' emotions. Anger causes poor circulation, which can have devastating effects on the entire body. It acts as a blockade, causing the body and mind to be less receptive to treatment. When agitated emotions subside and the patient is able to experience a sense of tranquility, recuperating is both easier and quicker. Anger and hatred are particularly detrimental to the healing process, and in fact, often worsen the problem.

3. Ignorance

When one is ignorant, one is unable to understand or see

things as they really are. Many of us are like this when it comes to illness. We are unable or unwilling to look at the root of the illness. Instead of pinpointing the true cause and effect that will help us to eradicate the illness, and instead of using wisdom to guide us to the proper care, we take a detour and become distracted by ineffective remedies. We sometimes look for a "quick fix," using unsubstantiated methods, unscientific therapies, and unsound doctors. Meanwhile, the illness is usually causing us both physical and psychological suffering. Using wisdom to investigate the actual cause of our illness will help us to set foot on the road to complete and long-lasting recovery.

While it is usually easy to detect the symptoms of a physical disease, we often remain ignorant of psychological diseases. They follow us like a shadow. We do not examine the constructs of our mind with wisdom and awareness, and poor psychological health follows. If we remain blind to our psychological diseases, the problems can compound and cause more severe sickness within our bodies. Modern scientists agree that anger, extreme happiness, anxiety, terror, sadness, and other emotions can impact one's physical well being. According to recent medical research, "When a person is unhappy, angry, or under pressure, his or her brain will release the hormones called adrenaline and nor-adrenaline, which can act as toxins." In addition, if the body is influenced by extreme emotions for a long period of time, the illness induced by the emotional imbalance or stress is harder to cure. For example, a digestive disorder rooted in a prolonged emotional condition is more difficult to cure than one caused by an external factor. There is scientific evidence, not just religious theory, that emotions indeed impact the healthy functioning of the body. Therefore, it is in our best interest to cultivate awareness of our emotional condition, handle our emotions well, and not become too attached to or controlled by them.

In Buddhism, there are eighty-four thousand methods that are used to cure eighty-four thousand illnesses. For instance, the Buddha taught that to eliminate greed, one can use the contemplation of impurity. Once a person meditates on impurity, he or she will experience a decrease in desire. The Buddha taught people afflicted with anger or hatred to practice universal kindness and compassion in order to reduce their hostility. When they feel themselves becoming angry, they should become mindful of the meaning of compassion. In doing so, they will understand that getting mad is not an appropriate or helpful response. Gradually, their angry words and thoughts will dissipate.

If people are ignorant, they should contemplate cause and effect and the law of impermanence to help them nurture the mindset of non-attachment. Nothing arises outside of dependent origination and nothing that arises will last forever; all phenomena will one day cease to exist. Since everything behaves like dust, which comes and goes, what is the purpose of being attached to it? Realizing there is no immunization for impermanence helps to reorient our minds from ignorance to wisdom and allows us to live with greater overall health.

Master Hanshan Deqing from the Ming Dynasty said, "No one can get sick, age, die, or be born for you. This suffering, only you must bear. All bitterness and sweetness one must go through on one's own." If we can accept the inevitability of suffering and impermanence with equanimity, it is like taking a dose of the finest medicine. Thus, when we adjust our emotions, subdue our temper, and act generously toward others, we will find our way through life's problems with more ease and reduce the chance of illness. If we apply these principles of Buddhist medicine to nurture our minds and restore our bodies, generosity will emerge out of greed, compassion will emerge out of anger, wisdom will emerge out of ignorance, and health will emerge out of sickness. When we treat the poisons of the mind and act with equanimity in all circumstances, there will be harmony of body and mind and disease will be kept at bay.

The Medicine of Buddhism

The occurrence of a disease is closely related to one's mental health, physical health, spiritual health, behavior, habits, living environment, and even the society and culture in which one lives. Harmonizing all of these elements and engaging in specific practices can help to bring about optimum health and prevent illness. Gaining awareness about the cause of illness and conducting our lives in a manner that nourishes and maintains long-term good health can drastically improve our overall well-being. The Buddha offers us several suggestions and practices that can serve as medicine for all aspects of our lives:

Practice Healthy Dietary Habits: A Chinese idiom states, "Troubles are caused by words flowing out of the mouth; illness is caused by food going into the mouth." Using caution and moderation in what we consume is an important practice for good health. Before consuming any food, we should determine if the food is fresh, if it is thoroughly cleaned, and what would be a reasonable amount to eat. The *Sutra of the Teachings Bequeathed by the Buddha* (*Chinese: I-chiao-ching Sutra*) states, "When we eat, we should regard our food as medicine, for consuming too much or too little is not healthy. A regular and proper dose can support our bodies, cure our hunger, relieve our thirst, and prevent us from becoming ill. Like bees gathering honey, they take what they need, but they don't consume the whole flower." As *Xingshi Chao* states, we should adjust the type of food we eat according to the season, consuming various combinations of food in order to maintain our body's equilibrium. Our bodies are susceptible to different ailments depending on the season, and a diet conscious of this fact offers a better chance of staying healthy.

The Regulation for Chan Monastery outlined five contemplations to be mindful of when we take our meals:

I consider the effort required
To grow and prepare the food;
I am grateful for its sources.
In observing my virtue;
If impeccable in mind and heart,
I shall deserve this offering.
I shall protect my heart
From being ensnared by faults;
I shall guard myself
Particularly against greed.
To cure my weakening body,
I shall consume this food as medicine.
To tread the path
Of spiritual cultivation;
I shall accept this food
As an offering.

One should maintain a balanced diet and approach food with a gracious attitude. When our bodies are given the right amount of food, our digestive organs will function properly, and our body's metabolism will be in prime condition, thus preventing digestive diseases and other health problems. Being mindful of and grateful for the food we consume contributes to the health of our mind as well as our body.

Meditation: Our mind is constantly exploring the world around us and, as a result, illusory thoughts are always arising and ceasing. Our over-active mind rarely gets a chance to rest. The constant stream of thoughts we experience can affect our ability to concentrate without interruption and can have a negative effect on our daily life. In addition to psychological health risks, one's physiology can also be adversely affected by an overwhelming amount of mental activity. The brain can cease to function properly due to our continual clutter of thoughts or an instance of severe mental excitation. For example, when one experiences a tremendous surprise, the face may appear discolored, the hands and feet become cold, and one's ability to concentrate normally will be impaired. However, if this person can take a deep breath to slow down the heartbeat and calm the emotions, the presence of tranquility will return the body to its normal state and the chance for harming any vital organs will decrease.

Through the meditative practice of breathing slowly and concentrating on the breath, one's psychological and physiological well-being can dramatically improve. In The Medicine Chan, written by a Japanese physician, three specific physical benefits derived from meditation were mentioned: 1) increased energy and a prolonged period of prime years, 2) improved blood circulation, and 3) a renewed endocrine system.[6] Through meditation, our body achieves a greater state of balance and our breathing becomes regulated. Our mind becomes focused, clear, and organized. Desires are dissolved and improper thoughts are eliminated. When our mind is clear and focused at all times, even as we walk, sit, and sleep, we will be calm and peaceful, which eventually results in a greater degree of overall health — both mental and physical. Master Tiantai Zhizhe recognizes the significant impact that meditation can have on overall health. He commented that if meditation is practiced on a regular basis and applied to daily occurrences with wisdom, all four hundred and four illnesses can be cured.

With a mind that is free from the exhaustion and confusion of constant thoughts, we can accomplish significant things in our lives, instead of merely thinking about doing so. Through acting, instead of just thinking, one can more authentically experience each moment and ultimately encounter the truth of life.

Paying Respect to the Buddha: The benefits of paying respect to the Buddha are numerous and come in many forms, nurturing both physical and mental health. Bowing to the Buddha increases the strength and flexibility of the body. When one bows, one's neck, hands, arms, waist, and legs stretch, giving the whole body an opportunity to exercise. By stretching the body, stiffness decreases and blood circulation increases, thus reducing the chance of becoming ill.

Although bowing results in distinct physical benefits, the act of bowing and the resulting benefits have more to do with our state of mind than our physical action. Our mental presence when bowing is of utmost importance. When we bow, we should show respect and sincerity, remaining deep in concentration as a slow bow is performed. As we pay respect in this manner, we should contemplate the Buddha then expand our focus to include unlimited Buddhas in all directions. When we pay respect to unlimited Buddhas, unlimited beings are benefited. Ourselves, the Buddha, in fact all true nature is empty. However, though empty, if one bows before the Buddha with a sincere and respectful heart, an amazing spiritual experience can take place. Contemplating the truth of emptiness teaches us to reorient our self-centered way of being and realize that the notion of self is merely illusory. Bowing, therefore, is performed not only to express our deepest gratitude to the Buddha and all Buddhas, it is also an effective way to eliminate our ignorance, decrease our attachment to self, dissolve the burden of karma, and cultivate our spiritual practice. As we can see, bowing is a health-giving gesture that nourishes both our body and mind.

Repentance: Confession is another practice that helps to restore and maintain our health. It is like clean water that washes away the dirt from one's heart and the dust from one's mind. A story about a Tang Master named Wuda offers us an example of how confession can be a healing agent. Master Wuda had a man killed in a previous life. Seeking revenge in future lives, the man who was killed was reborn as a sore on Master Wuda's foot. No doctor could cure the sore because it was a manifestation of Master Wuda's bad karma. After seeking guidance from an Arhat who helped him to realize his wrongdoing, Master Wuda repented with a sincere heart, cleansed his wound with pure water, and the sore disappeared. Only the heart of repentance could cure Master Wuda of his ailment. Thus, all of us should repent our mistakes and misdeeds to the Buddha and vow not to repeat the same behavior and create more bad karma. In addition, with the heart and mind of a bodhisattva, we may compassionately repent for all beings, thereby relieving their suffering as well as our own. Psychologically, repentance is believed to release impure thoughts and worrisome guilt that act like toxins in our bodies. It alleviates our mental burdens and reduces the potential for illness.

Reciting Mantras[7]: Mantras are powerful in curing diseases when recited with a sincere heart, deep concentration, and proper intentions. The *Great Compassion Mantra* and the

Medicine Buddha Mantra are two such examples. When recited, each mantra generates a tremendous amount of merit and has amazing healing and transforming effects.

Reciting the Buddha's Name: Many people are distressed by anxiety, agitation, improper desires, and delusional thoughts. These torments not only disturb our psychological well-being and eventually take a toll on our physical health, they also hinder our ability to perceive the truth of life and attain enlightenment. When we recite the name of the Buddha, the torment of improper and delusional thoughts will cease and our mental anguish will evaporate. The heart calms down, the mind is awakened and purified, and no greed, anger, ignorance, or other toxins will arise, thus giving us greater protection from illness and delivering us from our ignorance. Reciting the Buddha's name also helps us to reduce our bad karma, eliminating as many misdeeds as there are grains of sand in the Ganges. A Buddhist saying tells us, "Reciting the Buddha's name once can diminish one's bad karma, and bowing to the Buddha can increase one's good karma." Thus, reciting the Buddha's name is an effective practice for healing the distress of our minds and bodies, as well as benefiting our cultivation and awakening us to the truth of life.

Using the Dharma as Medicine: Our world is ailing from a broad range of modern diseases that, while not actually classified as standard medical illnesses, still cause overwhelming suffering and need to be treated. Some of these are environmental diseases, which include pollution, resource destruction, and loud noise, and societal diseases, including violence, harassment, materialism, kidnapping, and crime. There are also educational diseases, such as the physical and emotional abuse of students and the growing lack of respect for authority, and economic diseases, such as opportunism, greed, and corruption. There are also religious diseases, which could be explained as superstitious practices, religions that encourage harmful practices, and incorrect interpretations of religious concepts. Relationship diseases refer to infidelity, polygamy, and rape, and mental diseases include jealousy, distrust, and resentment. We may seek a doctor's help for physical illness, but the diseases listed above can only be cured by our own efforts to develop our character, cultivate our wisdom, and practice the Dharma. Buddhism can be used as a medicine to cure our minds of destructive and unhealthy thoughts, which create the conditions for all of the diseases mentioned above. A pure mind creates a pure world, and the wondrous Dharma is the perfect medicine to guide us to healthy thoughts, healthy behavior, and healthy lives.

In particular, the six paramitas[8] can be used to cure six kinds of diseases in Buddhism: 1) Generosity cures greed, 2) Observing the precepts cures violation of the precepts, 3) Tolerance cures hatred, 4) Diligence cures laziness, 5) Meditation cures the frenzied mind, and 6) Prajna (wisdom) cures ignorance. The medicine of the six paramitas enables us to treat our mind and generate peace and harmony in all aspects of our lives. When we embrace the Dharma, we can resolve the conflicts in our daily life with more ease and develop a healthy mind and a gracious character.

Master Shitou Wuji created a recipe of ingredients that can be used to turn an unhealthy mind into a healthy one. In the spirit of Master Shitou Wuji, I created my own recipe for health:

One strand of compassionate heart,
One slice of morality
And original nature,
A pinch of cherishing good fortune,
Three portions of

Gratitude and appreciation,
A complete package of
Sincere words and actions,
One piece of observation of
Precepts and upholding the Dharma,
One piece of humility,
Ten portions of diligence and frugality,
Combine all cause and effect,
And unlimited skillful means,
Establishing affinities,
The more the better!
Topped off with all your faith,
Vows, and practice.
Use the pot called magnanimity,
Use the heart called open-mindedness,
Don't burn it!
Don't let it dry out!
Lower your hot temper by three degrees,
(Mellow out and toss in a little gentleness.)
Put into a bowl and grind into small pieces.
(Like people entering each other's hearts and cooperating with each other.)
Think everything over three times,
Give encouragement as a pill,
Each day take this medicine three times,
Drink it down with the soup of
Love and compassion,
Remember when you take the medicine,
You cannot have clarity in speaking
While at the same time a muddled being.
Or benefit yourself at the expense of others.
Ambushing others from behind,
And harboring malice within,

Using a smile to masquerade the desire
To strike,
Or speaking from both sides of your mouth,
Creating disharmony just for the heck of it,
Refrain from engaging in the seven above,
Along with no jealousy or suspicion,
Use self-discipline,
And Truth to calm the troubled heart,
If you can do this, all ills will disappear.

The Contribution of Monastics to Medicine

In India, most monastics are well educated in the five sciences, especially in medicine, which they are required to study. Because knowledge of medicine is mandatory for monastics, throughout Buddhist history there are many well-known monastic physicians, medical scholars, and medical texts. For example, in the Buddhist sutras, we find countless references to and discussions about medicine. Evidence also demonstrates that Buddhism has made a significant contribution to the world of medicine not only through the development of respectable health theories and principles but also through actual practice. While by no means an exhaustive list, the following are brief accounts of Buddhist masters who have stood out in the history of Buddhist medicine.

In China, Master Buddhasimha was dedicated as the Honorable National Master of the East Jin Dynasty by Emperors Shi Le and Shi Hu. He was exceptionally skillful in reciting curative prayers and administering medicine. He tended to many patients who were paralyzed, in great pain, and were hopeless about finding a cure for their ailment. Master Buddhasimha never gave up on them, faithfully devoting his heart to caring for them as they suffered, prescribing the proper medication, and finding a lasting cure for their diseases.

Master Zhu Fatiao came to China from India, and stayed in Changshan Temple most of the time. He was quite famous for his ability to cure people, and patients journeyed hundreds of miles to seek his help. After skillfully diagnosing the problem and prescribing the appropriate treatment, nearly all of his patients were restored to good health.

Master Faxi lived during the Tang Dynasty. When he resided in the capital, he assumed full responsibility for all of his patients' needs and cared for them personally, including cleaning up their excrement. He never complained about this task or considered it filthy or difficult. On the contrary, he was always enthusiastic and joyful as he tended to his patients. Both the patients and fellow monastics praised his compassionate conduct. Master Faxi not only cured patients' physical diseases, he also patiently brought them the knowledge of the Dharma to comfort them when they were feeling hopeless or in pain.

Buddhists have also been credited for contributing to the cure of leprosy, a dangerous and contagious illness that often drove people away. However, many Buddhists chose not to avoid victims of leprosy, but instead, worked among them to help ease their suffering and cure their debilitating illness. Many monks put forth great effort to help leprosy patients, caring for them, encouraging them, changing their bandages, draining their infected sores, and doing their laundry. These people risked their lives by performing services that most people avoided. Their tenderness touched many people.

Conclusion

As we have discussed, numerous physical and mental diseases afflict us and cause us great suffering. While Buddhist medical theories acknowledge and treat the devastating effects of physical diseases, they regard diseases of the mind as the most destructive to health and happiness. According to Buddhism, people suffer from disease when they:

Cannot
Settle into peace of mind
Control anger
Resolve hatred
Calm a fearful heart
Dissolve sadness and worry
Cannot
Cease arguing
Stop competing
Practice humility and offer tolerance to others
Recognize when quietude is appropriate
Maintain a healthy balance of chi
Cannot
Endure life's difficulties
Lead a simple lifestyle
Practice proper etiquette
Cease their fear of death
Reorient erroneous perceptions

All of these diseases are caused by our rigid attachment — to an idea, belief, person, appearance, possession, emotion, status, or experience — to anything at all. If we can understand the true meaning of detachment and the true nature of emptiness and treat all illness with this awareness, we will then have the perfect, miracle medicine to remove the roots of disease. Both the body and the mind need to be taken care of, and the medicine of Buddhism is the ideal remedy. Use the Dharma to heal your mind, and the path of true health will open up for you. I wish you health and happiness!

Ganges River

Notes

1 The Tripitaka is the canon of Buddhist teachings, including Sutras (sermons of the Buddha), the Vinaya (precepts and rules of Buddhist discipline), and the Abhidharma (commentary on the Buddha's teachings).

2 Medicine is one of the five sciences whose study is mandatory for monastics. The other four are language, arts and mathematics, logic, and the philosophy of Buddhism.

3 According to Chinese medicine, chi is the energy or life force that circulates throughout the body; this vital power is believed to flow throughout the entire universe.

4 In practicing the Middle Way, one avoids both extremes of indulgence and asceticism.

5 Sometimes referred to as "temptations" or "afflictions," these mind-torments, e.g. greed, anger, sloth, jealousy, and many others, inhibit one from residing in true, original, pure mind.

6 System of glands that secrete hormones directly into the lymph or bloodstream.

7 Also known as a "dharani," a mantra is a powerful spiritual practice of reciting a word, sound, or verse, used to cultivate wisdom, deepen concentration, and effect a change in consciousness.

8 Literally meaning "crossing over to the other shore," paramitas are the core virtues of the bodhisattva path.

About
Venerable Master Hsing Yun

Venerable Master Hsing Yun was born in Jiangdu, Jiangsu province, China, in 1927. Tonsured under Venerable Master Zhikai at age twelve, he became a novice monk at Qixia Vinaya School and Jiaoshan Buddhist College. He was fully ordained in 1941, and is the 48th Patriarch of the Linji (Rinzai) Chan school.

He went to Taiwan in 1949 where he undertook to revitalizing Chinese Mahayana Buddhism on the island with a range of activities novel for its time. In 1967, he founded the Fo Guang Shan (Buddha's Light Mountain) Buddhist Order, and had since established more than a hundred temples in Taiwan and on every continent worldwide. Hsi Lai Temple, the United States Headquarters, was built outside Los Angeles in 1988.

At present , there are nearly two thousand monks and nuns in the Fo Guang Shan Buddhist Order. The organization also oversees sixteen Buddhist colleges; five publishing houses including, Buddha's Light Publishing, Hsi Lai University Press; four universities, one of which is Hsi Lai University in Los Angeles; a secondary school; a satellite television station; an orphanage; and a nursing home for the elderly.

A prolific writer and an inspiring speaker, Master Hsing Yun has written many books on Buddhist sutras and a wide spectrum of topics over the past five decades. Most of his speeches and lectures were compiled into essays defining Humanistic Buddhism and outlining its practice. Some of his writings and lectures are translated into different languages, such as English, Spanish, German, Russian, Japanese, Korean, etc.

The Venerable Master is also the founder of Buddha's Light International Association, a worldwide organization of lay Buddhists dedicated to the propagation of Buddhism, with over 130 chapters and more than a million in membership.

English Publication by
Venerable Master Hsing Yun

Buddha's Light Publishing:
1. Between Ignorance and Enlightenment (I)
2. Between Ignorance and Enlightenment(II)
3. The Awakening Life
4. Fo Guang Study
5. Sutra of the Medicine Buddha
   - with an Introduction, Comments and Prayer
6. From the Four Noble Truths to the Four Universal Vows
   - An Integration of the Mahayana and Theravada Schools
7. On Buddhist Democracy, Freedom and Equality
8. Of Benefit to Oneself and Others
   - A Critique of the Six Perfections

Wisdom Publications:
9. Only a Great Rain
   - A Guide to Chinese Buddhist Meditation
10. Describing the Indescribable
    - A Commentary on the Diamond Sutra

Weatherhill, Inc.:
11. Being Good
    - Buddhist Ethics for Everday Life
12. Lotus in a Stream
    - Basic Buddhism for Beginners

iUniverse.com, Inc.:
13. Humble Table, Wise Fare
    - Gift for Life

Peter Lang Publishing:
14. The Lion's Roar

Hsi Lai University Press:
15. Handing Down the Light
16. Perfectly Willing
17. Happily Ever After
18. How I Practice Humanistic Buddhism
19. Where is Your Buddha Nature
20. The Carefree Life
21. Humble Table, Wise Fare
    - Hospitality for the Heart (I)
22. Humble Table, Wise Fare
    - Hospitality for the Heart (II)
23. Cloud and Water
    - An Interpretation of Chan Poems
24. Contemporary Thoughts on Humanistic Buddhism

Fogung Cultural Enterprise Co., Ltd.
25. Where there is Dharma,
    There is a Way
26. The Everlasting Light:
    Dharma Thoughts of Master Hsin Yun

About
Buddha's Light Publishing
and Fo Guang Shan
International Translation Center

In 2001, Buddha's Light Publishing was established to publish Buddhist books translated by Fo Guang Shan International Translation Center as well as other valuable Buddhist works. Buddha's Light publishing is committed to building bridges between East and West, Buddhist communities, and cultures. All proceeds from our book sales support Buddhist propagation efforts.

As long as Venerable Master Hsing Yun has been a Buddhist monk, he has had a strong belief that books and other documentations of the Buddha's teachings is the way to unite us emotionally, help practice Buddhism at a higher altitude, and continuously define as well as challenge our views on living our lives.

In 1996, the Fo Guang Shan International Translation Center was established with this goal in mind. This marked the beginning of a string of publications translated into various languages from the Master's original writings in Chinese. Presently, several translation centers have been set up worldwide. Centers in Los Angeles and San Diego, USA; Sydney, Australia; Berlin, Germany; Argentina; South Africa; and Japan; coordinate translation or publication projects.

Notes

Notes

Notes

Notes

Notes

Notes

Notes